C. Northcote Parkinson needs little introduction to his very large number of readers. He taught in universities as far apart as Illinois and Liverpool, Harvard and Malaya. He wrote the world-famous *Parkinson's Law* and many other books which have sold in millions.

M.K. Rustomji was a top executive in the Tata Engineering and Locomotive Company, TELCO, one of the largest organisations of its kind in the world, before turning to consulting and writing. His numerous books on Management remain in great demand in countries such as U.K., U.S.A., India, Spain, Japan, etc. Rustomji published twenty books in collaboration with C. Northcote Parkinson and co-authored a popular book on health with the world-famous Dr. Christian Barnard. He thrice won the Escorts Book Award for the best Management Book of the Year. He was also assigned the prestigious and path-breaking task of reorganisation and streamlining the entire administration of Andhra Pradesh. One of Rustomji's books was made into a prize winning film by the Government of India.

Comments on Parkinson-Rustomji Bestsellers

"The attraction is not only the universality of message, but also the eye-catching way in which it is presented."
Financial Times, London.

"Effective and attractive . . . I am issuing instructions to have a few copies available for all the companies in our group."
J.R.D. Tata.

"I have not seen anything of its kind nearly as good."
Lord Pilkington, Chairman, Pilkington Ltd.

"Excellent . . . unquestionably worthwhile." David Rockefeller

"Must for every executive." *The Times of India*

". . . most interesting and rewarding." Russi Mody,
Former Chairman, Tata Iron & Steel Co. Ltd. (TISCO)

"Scintillating — no (other) books bring out the philosophy of management half so simply." *Financial Express*

UNDERSTANDING MANAGEMENT

The Key to better results in your organization

C. NORTHCOTE PARKINSON
M. K. RUSTOMJI

Illustrated by
R.K. Laxman

VISION
BOOKS

www.visionbooksindia.com

First Published 1988
10th Printing 2013

ISBN 10: 81-7094-441-4
ISBN 13: 978-81-7094-441-6

Published by
Vision Books Pvt. Ltd.
(Incorporating Orient Paperbacks & CARING imprints)
24 Feroze Gandhi Road, Lajpat Nagar 3
New Delhi 110024 (India).

Phone: (+91-11) 26836470/80
E-mail: visionbk@vsnl.com
visionbooks@gmail.com

. Printed at
Rashtra Rachna Printers
C-88, Ganesh Nagar, Pandav Nagar Complex,
Delhi-110092, India.

Contents

Preface

Over the last hundred years or so there has been a change in the fabric of society. Society, which once consisted of individuals working mainly for themselves, now consists of organizations of all types: factories, government departments, hospitals, universities, hotels, armed forces, airlines, multinational banks, communication and data processing units and so on. If these organizations are well managed, it follows that the individuals who make up our society will prosper. Conversely, if these organizations are not well managed, individuals will suffer. Therefore good management is the key to the well-being of our present-day society and this book is all about various aspects of effective management.

It is designed for the manager at various levels and also for one who is aiming to reach the top and has come, perhaps, within sight of it. For the ambitious reader who sees himself as the chief executive the first question is whether he wants the responsibility or whether he merely wants the salary and prestige. There is no situation more miserable than that of having the position but not the qualities of a chief executive. To be happy at the top you need courage, stamina and a strong sense of dedication. There is a price to be paid for success and you need to be clear in your mind that the price is one you are willing to pay. Let us suppose that you know the price and are still resolved on reaching the summit. You are confident of success and will not endure to see someone else fumbling over a task for which you feel especially qualified. You know the trade and have a gift for organization. You mean to reach the top.

One essential quality you will need, in that case, is a sense of dedication — but to what? There are people in the world who devote their lives to religion or public administration. There are folks who sacrifice all for the sake of exploration or science. Some give their lives for the Marxist cause or in defence of the downtrodden and oppressed. So, what is our comparable aim in business? Our aim is to supply the world with good, well-made, comfortable and sturdy shoes (or overcoats or vests) at a fair price and in sufficient quantity. Assuming office as the chief executive, you have undertaken to do just that, not for your own profit, not in the name of any ideology but simply as a matter of trade. There are, as we shall see, a number of other purposes you must serve; but the above-mentioned purpose is paramount and should be the aim of every honest manufacturer or merchant. It is an aim, moreover, which only a fool can despise. Looking at the people in a city street, the missionary may say "I shall convert them to the true faith", the politician will say "I shall persuade them to vote for the right party" and the revolutionary will say "I shall show them how to overthrow tyranny". The industrialist's claim "I provided them with their underwear" may, by comparison, seem

humble, mundane and almost laughable. But there are two points
to note about the manufacturer's quiet remark. First of all, his
claim is a matter of fact, not of opinion. He has done what he has
set out to do. The idealists tell us that they mean to save the
world, a promise for the future and one which they may or may
not fulfil. While they merely promise, the industrialist has performed. In the second place, the maker of underwear has done
people a good service and one which only a fool would question.
No one has been compelled to purchase his products, nobody is
forced to wear them. All he has done is to make them available,
and we should clearly be the worse off had he failed in his task.
There is no such certainty about the idealist's claims on our grati-
tude. How do we know that the doctrine preached is the true
faith? How do we know that one political party is wiser than any
other? How do we know that a revolution will not make things
worse? At the end of his career the manufacturer of underwear
can claim to have worked effectively in the cause of cleanliness,
hygiene and comfort. Can the idealists claim as much? Can they,
in some instances, claim anything at all?

There are people in the world who will plunge society into bloodshed so as to bring about some future and doubtful Utopia. There are people who throw bombs and commit air piracy in the name of this cause and that. The industrialist, by comparison, has been a general benefactor and has little reason to be ashamed of himself. Promising a great deal less, he has done a great deal more. Nor has his task been a simple one. He has to transact business so as to satisfy his suppliers, his shareholders, his employees, his retailers and the public. To enable all to benefit from his work is incomplete until he has also satisfied the national government, the tax collector, the local government and rate-collector, the trade associations and trade unions, the health inspector and the chamber of commerce. In the world of free enterprise the industrialist is expected to perform a daily miracle. Under a socialist government he would enjoy a monopoly, where no other products are placed on the market. Under a communist government his employees would not be allowed to go on strike. In contrast, the industrialist in a free enterprise has to satisfy everybody,

AN EXECUTIVE HAS TO SATISFY EVERYBODY

offering a good price for his raw materials, announcing a fair dividend, paying good wages and marketing an attractive product at a price which people can afford to pay. If he can do all that he has no reason to feel ashamed of himself. And that is the task to which the chief executive is committed.

Among political theorists we have seen disagreement over the basic question: does the State exist to serve the individual or does the individual exist to serve the State? Should the State provide for the citizen or should the subject lay down his life for the Emperor? We have also heard the same sort of argument applied to the factory. Does it exist to provide a dividend to the shareholders? Does it exist to provide employment for the workers? Or should it rather exist as a branch of the government? Each of these ideas must be discussed at the outset. Not only are all the theorists mistaken but they make the same mistake — that of ignoring the craftsman's real loyalty, which is or should be to his craft. The purpose of the craftsman may be to make good shoes and boots. Replace him by a factory and the purpose is still the same: to do honest work at a fair price. The industrialist has many people to satisfy, as we have seen, but his main responsibility is toward the product he places on the market. Neither he nor his employees must ever think that the factory exists to provide the shareholders with a dividend. Least of all, does it exist for the glory of the State. Its loyalty should be, above all, to its products and its reputation for good workmanship and value. Once people are allowed to deviate from that central purpose, all is lost. Incidentally, when one loses all his sense of pride in work, the wages, the dividends, the taxes and rates are also lost. Left without the right aim and object the factory will soon be no more than a heap of ruins.

As chief executive in the enterprise, you must always keep the end in view. It cannot be a selfish aim. If your object is to gain a more important position and you are using your present appointment as a mere rung on the ladder, your intention will become obvious and you will never have an effective team. Why should other people seek to advance your career? That is not a purpose they will accept. Give them a higher aim (like the goal of the

HIGH PRODUCTION MAKES PEOPLE HAPPY

honest craftsman), and you can all work together. In that cause
you can collect, train and inspire a team which will respond to
your leadership. The object of this book is to show how you can
best set about it. Herein lie the secrets of management, the mistakes to avoid, the points to remember, and the tricks of the
trade. Your art must be in working through other men and
women, not in doing the work yourself. Your task will be to think
and foresee, organize and plan. Here is a collection of basic principles and detailed practices which will ensure that you achieve
the best results. One of the most useful conclusions is that you will
not be working to make your employees happy. If you do that
you will probably ruin the business, employees and all. Happiness
is seldom achieved by those who go in search of it. For most of us,
happiness is a by-product, achieved when we are aiming at something else; for example, when we are trying to market a good
product at a fair price. When our organization is efficient enough
to do that, we shall find, perhaps to our astonishment, that we
have achieved much more, including happiness.

1

Authority and Leadership

As you approach the summit of an organization, you must ask yourself whether or not you want to find yourself alone on that pinnacle. You have so far known yourself to be ambitious. You have wanted success. It seems to be almost within your grasp. Now that you can see what it involves, are you still intent on that last promotion? There is only one man at the top. He has sacrificed a great deal to be where he is. Are you willing to make the sacrifices; and if so, why? You should not want power just for the love of it: your aim should be greater than that. The sense of power will not give you satisfaction for long. Your pleasure in that will soon diminish, leaving you with a heavy sense of responsibility, and a burden which you will always have to carry. You must decide now whether or not you are willing to pay the price, knowing that you might be happier, that life would certainly be easier, in a lower position or in a smaller firm. And do not imagine that you can share your burden with a board of directors. The board is necessary and its members are the men who, in their last resort, may ask you to resign. But while the enterprise continues to show a profit, the directors will not interfere with the business. Nor will the chairman encourage them to ask too many questions. In the normal course, a strong chairman will support the chief executive, on whom the main responsibility must rest.

Once you are at, or even near, the top, there are a number of mistakes to avoid, the first being to make yourself too remote. To emphasize the gulf between you and former rivals — men alongside whom you have worked, perhaps for years — you may entrench yourself behind too many outer offices and personal assistants. Some such policy may even be expected of you. But there are real dangers in losing touch with your subordinates. Find subtle means to know what is going on. While your main function should be to deal only with broad lines of policy, it is advantageous to go into details from time to time, not so often as to upset the department heads, but often enough to show that you are not blind to all that is happening. General directives may have to be issued but remember that they lose impact as they descend through the various levels, sometimes giving the wrong impression or no impression at all.

Another temptation to guard against is abusing your power, wielding the big stick in person. This is always a mistake and for a variety of reasons; the first being that you cannot be everywhere at once and that most of the work must be done in your absence. One remedy for the slackness that may prevail necessarily owing to this is to set up a target of performance and enthuse everybody in an achievement which they can regard as theirs, not merely yours. A second remedy lies in your own example, which should be one of cheerful determination. A third remedy lies in projecting your own high morale by means of the telephone, which is more effective than the written message. Another temptation that afflicts many chief executives is worrying too much, thinking of all the mistakes that may be made and of all the difficulties they may encounter. Chances are, with a sufficient amount of activity in all directions, a few mistakes will hardly be noticed and many problems will solve themselves before they even reach your desk. Aim at success, not at the avoidance of error. Cherish the people who work for you and encourage them to use their brains. Do not let them come to you asking 'What shall we do?' Make them bring you the problem together with their proposed solution: 'We mean to do this. Is it agreed?' The final result will be that they will identify themselves with the general effort, claim all the success for themselves and fail to acknowledge that you have done anything; and that is exactly how it should be.

All Good Leaders Have Certain Common Principles of Management

Good managers are cast in different moulds — gay or colourless, garrulous or reticent, dominating or self-effacing — but, above all, they are efficient. Generals Marshall and MacArthur for instance, are both very fine leaders, despite their diametrically opposing personalities.

What, then, makes this diverse bunch so good? Certain common methods and practices are found to be the reasons:

- Effective executives keep a strict control over their time.

- Their focus is on *outward* contribution. They achieve results not by slogging, but through good, pertinent direction.

- They build on strengths — their own strengths, the strength of their colleagues, and that of their superiors and their subordinates. They neither lament nor condone weaknesses.

- They concentrate on the few major areas where good performance can produce outstanding results. They do first things first and second things preferably not at all.

- They know that to make many decisions fast is to make wrong decisions: what is needed are a few but fundamental decisions.

- They delegate as much as they can so as to keep themselves free to think about the future plans of their organizations.

One Boss . . .

. . . and one Boss only. That's basic in management. Unless you have this, you will never have proper discipline. In a situation where a person has more than one immediate boss, he may justify

his non-action to one boss by saying that he is working for the other boss. After all, we are only human. And bosses who, strange as it may seem, are human too, can be played off, one against the other. But it's entirely in order to have functional relationships with many people. The finance manager can help you as far as finance is concerned, the personnel manager for personnel policies, the purchase manager of purchases and so on. But these fellows are virtually advisers, not bosses. So if you've done something wrong and have to be hauled up — only one man can do it, and that's your boss.

Why Do They Want Power?

Some people have an irresistible urge for it. It's like a ravenous hunger. For some, power is the heady feeling of wielding influence

over others and they feel it's completely intoxicating to know that a large number of people are dependent on them. People are willing to do anything to obtain power. They will suffer hardship, work enormously long hours, give up their leisure, ruin their health, forget about their families, all for the sake of power.

If you want power because it gives you the means to do good work, then you deserve to have it. But if it is just to give you a feeling of authority and superiority, then you lack the essential quality of an executive.

It's a Big Responsibility

Responsibility involves making proper use of money which belongs to other people. For instance, if an existing machine is running smoothly, it takes a lot of courage to replace it with a new machine which is more expensive, especially when the pay-off on the new machine will only materialize over a long period. In the same way, it is not easy to spend large sums of money on

research and development when there might not be results for years on end. These decisions become especially difficult in the face of ever-changing modern technology which quickly makes expensive equipment obsolete. These are areas where the courage and capabilities of a manager are fully tested.

Similarly, a manager has to have courage in deciding what tasks *not* to tackle and sticking to his decision. Often, managers tend to take on far too much. This makes everybody happy; but, of course, the drawback is that nothing ever gets done properly. Courage is an important managerial quality.

You Have to Decide

Do you want to be a follower or a boss? A leader has to make plans, give orders and see that the work is done. He is well paid; he has power, authority and respect. But he has certain very definite obligations. There are occasions when he has to put his work before his family, his hobbies and his friends — very often, even his health. He must set the example. He's on duty all the time. A leader also has to be on a constant alert both on and off the job. He cannot expect to be a mere 9 to 5 working man; nor are carefree weekends always available to him. For there's always the possibility of a strike somewhere or an electric power breakdown. Certain bills have to be paid and the money just has to be produced. One mistake and the competition can overwhelm him. Being boss is certainly no bed of roses. You have to decide if you want to pay the price.

How Useful Are Board Meetings?

As the functions of ownership of an organization and its control become increasingly exclusive, the representatives of the owners, namely the board of directors, have less and less influence insofar as the day-to-day functioning of the organization is concerned. Indeed, most organizations have nowadays become so complex that they can be run only by full-time executives.

- Therefore a board cannot and must not be the directing body which the law considers it to be. The way in which it might be useful is as an organ of review. Only in a managerial or financial crisis does it become an organ of action and even then, it is for purpose of removing the existing executives who have failed.

- In some organizations, the board of directors consists of both full-time and part-time directors. In such cases, the great difficulty is that of finding good and capable part-time men to sit on the boards and take their membership seriously.

- Part-time directors necessarily know little or nothing about the company which they represent. They certainly cannot know much, because board meetings are infrequently held for an hour or two every month. So they are seldom in a position to intervene effectively.

8

- Where there are full-time and part-time directors on a board, you will not find full-time directors bringing up important controversial matters because that may show up their own performance and that of their organization badly in front of the part-time directors.

- A task can be done in many different ways, but since the chairman is the man responsible for the performance of the organization, what he thinks should carry the day. The chairman should have the other directors properly at heel, otherwise, a lot of time will be wasted and an enormous amount of unnecessary information will be asked for.

- It might even be a good thing to have a board staffed almost entirely by outside persons who know little about the details of the organization. In such cases the very remoteness of the outside board members might make them see things on an overall basis. They will perceive in terms of overall objectives and plans and will ask questions relating to concepts and principles. In fact, they may be in a position to bring out points which the inside full-time executives, who have their noses too close to the problem, have failed to notice.

Well Looked After

But this does not mean that the executives who have risen to great heights are anxious to be treated as something exceptional and special. They realize that they must not lose the contacts which they used to have with their employees. What often happens is that when someone becomes head of an organization, everyone seems to think that he should be put in an aseptic room. The result is that he is unable to see what is going on right under his very nose. Old colleagues and friends treat him as if he were a visitor from another planet. Somehow he does not get the information he used to have. He tends to lose touch. He no longer feels the pulse of his employees. As you can see the top officer has a difficult task. He has good reasons for keeping everyone at arm's length.

He must not get too friendly with his subordinates. But at the same time he must keep in touch with his men so that he knows what is going on.

Minute Specks of Dust

Why should the Big Boss take this trouble? Because he's wise enough to know that with an occasional getting down to details with the industrial engineering staff, much information can be obtained. But remember, he does this very rarely — only once in a while, for it is essential for him never to get bogged down by too many details.

If people in an organization know that the boss himself, at any time, is liable to get down to details, and in any area, it tends to keep everybody on their toes.

Through having the details of routines examined step by step, form by form, one finds that a lot of unnecessary work has crept in. So by arranging to get the details of an organization examined,

10

many of the routines of an organization can be streamlined and much unnecessary work can be eliminated.

The re-examination of procedures often results in the development of a system which is self-checking and where details are looked after automatically without the boss having to deal with them personally.

But these results can only come about if the boss himself occasionally arranges to go into details. So you see how important it is to examine the minute specks of dust on the floor!

Elements of Leadership

Interruptions are fatal

- A study of twelve chief executives was made in Sweden. It was found that not one of the twelve executives, whose work was studied in some detail, •was able to work consecutively for more than twenty minutes at a time; they were being constantly interrupted by one thing or another. Nothing worth-

11

while can ever be done unless one has a long stretch of uninterrupted time to do it. Otherwise, the time spent is just wasted and one has to start all over again.

An assistant to his men

- The old concept of the strong manager having everything under his control is now fast dying away. The IBM Company, which has done a great deal of research on management, has defined the manager's task in relation to his subordinates as an 'assistant' to them. IBM has found that a manager is most effective and produces the best results if he considers his main function as that of helping his subordinates to do their jobs. After all, a manager himself can, at best, only do the work of just one man. But he becomes more effective if he ensures that all his numerous subordinates are helped in every way in their work. This should be his main function and it will produce far better results than if he spends his time concentrating on his own work.

Executive qualities

- A manager should do his best to prevent people "hanging around", waiting to see him and he should not let the big bosses or VIPs waste his staff's time either.

- An executive must know that if he has really understood a subject, nothing is so complicated that it cannot be explained in less than ten minutes.

- If a mistake has been made, an executive should spend a long time discussing it to make sure that the mistake does not happen again. But when things turn out right, he shouldn't waste time trying to get to know the details.

- Another thing is to learn to say 'NO', and this is very difficult because one is often under great pressure: both personal and otherwise. But an executive can never be really effective unless he learns to say 'NO' when the occasion demands it.

12

- An executive must have the right values. He must know that nothing is more important than his men — after all, they're the people who turn out the products. The problems of his staff — be they personal or professional — should be accorded the highest priority. Procrastination in this matter must inevitably lead to a loss of efficiency.

Appointing Staff

When it is a question of promoting staff to higher positions, a good executive does not spare himself. He realizes this is an area where any amount of time and energy expended would be well rewarded. After all, future generals are going to be chosen from today's colonels: so if the chief executive of the future is going to be good, no pains should be spared in choosing the colonels.

13

- He never takes personal considerations into account except where they are likely to affect his performance. To him what matters is what a man can do. He realizes that each 'people' decision is a gamble. But, basing the gamble on a man's proven capabilities, it becomes at least a rational gamble.

- Very often, only one man is best qualified for a particular post and the good leader has no hesitation in appointing him to that post, regardless of the fact that pulling him out of his present set-up may cause inconveniences to that set-up. In the final analysis, no one is indispensable. The lower echelons will soon sort themselves out and the organization will have placed a good man where he can be most effective.

- It is important to realize that a good executive — no matter how well-paid he might be — probably costs much less in the long run than a poor one. Remember, an executive normally handles big issues involving large sums of money — and this fact alone would far outweigh the additional salary he might be getting as compared to that of a second-rate executive.

Management committed by its own mistakes

- Management, like every other decision-making body, is committed by its own mistakes. If it makes a mistake in promoting a man, it should not fire him because his subsequent

performance shows that he should never have been given the promotion. It may not be the fault of the man that he performs badly: the requirements of the job may be quite simply beyond his capacity and talent. If he does not fit satisfactorily into his new slot, management must undoubtedly remove him as quickly as possible. But in such cases, management has a moral responsibility to absorb the employee who is otherwise loyal and has been with them for many years, in a post where his capabilities can be better utilized.

Teamwork

- No matter what the textbooks say, well-managed companies do not place all the responsibility upon a single chief executive. Even Henry Ford, who was quite a despot in his way, commented on the subject of running an organization: 'It must not be the job of one man; but should be the job of a team acting together.'

- But it is important for management to realize that for any team to be effective, every member should have a clearly assigned and defined role. Good teamwork entails considerable organization and precision in the individual assignment of work: it must be a 'team', not a committee. Each member of the team should have a definite area of work assigned to him in

which he makes the final decision and for which he is responsible. There should be no collective responsibility; if everyone is responsible, no one is responsible. There can be consultations with the team but the decision should be made by a team member singly.

- The second requirement is that there should be no passing the buck from one member of the team to another. At the same time, whenever any one of them takes a decision in his area it becomes the decision of the team as a whole.

- If work has to be done effectively, a team must be small in number. One of the largest directing teams of an organization is that of Standard Oil which has fourteen persons. But normally the most effective results can be obtained if a team consists of only about three or four members.

- A team does not normally make a good supervisor. Wherever possible, people should be asked to report not to a team but to an individual member of a team. Assisting and teaching are best performed by an individual rather than by a team. If an organization is going to grow — and every organization must grow or else it will stagnate — then the management of one man, or a handful of men, must be replaced by a proper management team. The overall boss must analyse the key business needs and also his own personality and capability. There will always be key activities that do not fit the top man; activities that others can do better. It follows then, that others should do them.

Ralph Cordiner, the legendary Chairman of General Electric, always made the point that a chief executive should arrange his duties in such a manner that, three to four years after he is in the saddle, there should be at least three men in the organization team who are trained and ready to replace him. He also said that where the emoluments of the chief executive are very much greater than those of his next in command, it would indicate that there is something wrong with the organization and that no proper provision has been made for an orderly transition.

16

Stop an Activity ·If It Is Not Entirely Essential

A question which an effective manager should ask of his various tasks is: 'If we did not do this work or service, or make this product in the first place, would we have taken it up now?'

If the answer is no, then a strong-minded manager should do everything possible to drop the project, in spite of the considerable amount of time, money, prestige and energy that has already been spent on it.

One of the reasons for the great success of the well-known Du Pont Company is that the Company has learnt to abandon a process or a product before it begins to decline. They have always felt that it is useless to spend time, effort and money on something that is not right up with the market or ahead of the market. They have always been willing to sacrifice large sums of money to adhere to this policy.

You Just Can't . . .

. . . act like a policeman over each and every one of your men. You can't check exactly how much time he takes in the lavatory; how much time he is taking over his tea. You can't always watch

to see when a machine tool is ticking over and when it is actually cutting material. What is the alternative? It is sympathetic and understanding leadership. If a manager can earn the respect of his workmen and convince them that he is trying his best to give them a fair deal, then good discipline, good behaviour and conscientious work will follow automatically. Police methods are of little use in the long run.

You May Be the Boss . . .

. . . but try to carry it lightly. No one likes being ordered about and having people in authority over them. So remember, even if you are the boss, take it easy. Don't throw your weight around. One of the main tasks of a manager is to motivate people: to make them want to work. But instead of this you'll be surprised at the number of managers who only succeed in discouraging their men with their dictatorial attitude.

Eye on the Target

That's what you should always have. Nothing matters except hitting the bull's eye. There is nothing like concentrating on your object to get results. But you will be amazed at the number of times this principle is broken; and how often one is led away on to numerous side issues.

The amount of time and effort executives waste on irrelevant pursuits is astonishing. They sometimes make journeys, attend lunches and meetings which are irrelevant to the main objective. Much more important, you'll be surprised to know about the numerous companies that have been badly hit through branching out into activities way out of their main line of business. We should always keep our eye on the main target. Concentration on our objective is the key to success.

No other principle of effectiveness is violated as constantly as

this basic principle of concentration. This is true not only of businesses but also government departments, universities, hospitals and in fact every organization of our society. We are similarly profligate with respect to managerial staff activities — and managerial staff is a very expensive commodity. Our motto seems to be 'Let's do a bit of everything'. As with other expenditure, we scatter our efforts. It has been found that in many businesses 90% of the significant results are being produced by only about 10% of the events. Yet this point has not been brought home at all.

Far better results would be produced if managers concentrated on the areas which produced results rather than doing things just because they have been done previously. Do not think that it would be a let-down to discontinue something which has been done for years. Neither is it good to do things simply out of prestige.

The other important step for effectiveness is to do one thing at a time. Do first things first and other things, if possible, not at all. Or let someone else do them. An executive who does too many things at the same time will not succeed in doing anything really well. Things which are really worth doing requires adequate time. So one must develop the self-discipline to make time to do the really important things. In a circus a juggler might play with a dozen balls at a time but, eventually, one is bound to drop. So it will be the same with the executive who tries to do too many jobs at the same time. Sooner or later things will go wrong.

We Can't All Have This . . .

. . . lovely sands, beautiful women, clear blue water. But do you know how Henry Kaiser managed it? His secret was the telephone. He seldom wrote letters but he had a close grip over his whole empire from Honolulu. The telephone can give immediate clarification. Decisions can be taken straight away. We cannot all be Henry Kaisers but we can certainly make more use of the telephone. Do this and you might also end up in Honolulu!

Don't Cross Your Bridges . . .

. . . before you have to. In the same way, don't start worrying about errors before you make them. Errors very often have a tendency of looking after themselves. You will often find that a go-ahead concern with plenty of drive and initiative, does a

sufficiently large amount of business to absorb most of the mistakes that are made. Keep forging ahead and get things done. Forget about the mistakes you might make. The important thing is to judge the percentage of somebody's total successes against his errors.

It Is Not the Effort but the Results That Matter

This is the chief executive; he is flooded with papers — with work. He's very busy. But 'what is he contributing? Hardly anything. He has no time to think and plan ahead. No time to innovate. He is much too busy just working.

The thing to remember is that an organization is not an end in itself. The justification for its existence is the contribution it makes. The danger is that the bigger an organization grows the more its people will think about the problems connected with the 'inside' details of the organization itself: their prospects, their promotion, their wages, their quarrels, office space and tea-breaks. Executives look into these problems at the expense of their real task — which is to make the organization more productive and more useful. For example, unless the customer is satisfied,

everything collapses and there would be no point carrying on at all. The quality of the product made and the service given are also very important. The smaller the organization and the fewer the people, the less emphasis there is on 'inside' things. So smaller organizations are better able to make more contributions.

Contribution is what is important

There should be a distinction between effort, work, and the results of that work. Many executives might put in an enormous amount of work but the actual result or contribution of this might be very little indeed. The executive might be working only on matters connected to the 'inside' details of his own particular department or organization. He may be dealing with problems that inevitably arise due to having a mass of 'interpersonal' problems. But an executive only becomes valuable when he looks 'outside' his organization and becomes interested, not just in carrying on, but in contributing something new. It is really this that justifies his being on the payroll; not the fact that he is in charge of a big department of an organization. The important thing is what the department or organization produces by way of results; what it contributes.

HE IS CONTRIBUTING ALL RIGHT!

Doesn't Exist for its own sake

This principle applies to all organizations. For example, the aim of an income-tax department, clearly, is not to run the department for convenience of its own employees but to collect taxes, and to collect them with the least amount of bother to the tax payer. That surely is the contribution of an income-tax department. Similarly a hospital does not exist for its own sake but for the manner in which it treats its patients.

There is also the example of some embassies of the major powers which are so badly organized that the ambassadors spend all their time just to get to know their staff and run the embassy. This way, they have little time for their real job, which is to get acquainted with the country to which they are accredited and to explain their own countries to it. So, in reality, such ambassadors contribute very little — they do little by way of real work although they are in fact working very hard.

Get work done 'outside'

A manager should never spend more than about a tenth of his time in dealing with problems arising out of his work force. Where more of his time is spent on such matters, his performance will be impeded. His work force is probably too large. The more people one has on the 'outside', such as specialists and consultants, the better it is because it gives the manager more time to get on with his real tasks rather than with the problems brought about by the size of his organization. The well-known Chrysler Corporation was very successful in its policy of having as much work done outside as possible. In fact at one stage everything was subcontracted except for the assembly of the car and the manufacture of the engine. And this policy made Chrysler one of the most dynamic automobile manufacturers in the USA. It enabled its top executives to concentrate on the things that really mattered — the 'outside' things.

It's performance that matters

Capable executives know that their subordinates are there to do their jobs and not to please them. For example, the manager of a theatre company has to put up with all the tantrums of the leading star. It might be a difficult thing to do but if the star performs well, then both the manager and the star have earned their pay. It is not pleasing people that matters. It is performance that counts. A teacher in a school or university may be unpleasant and difficult, but if he is a good teacher then the principal of the school or the dean of the college has earned his pay by putting up with the teacher. A good leader should never ask: 'How does somebody get along with me?' The first question should be 'What does he contribute?' Or 'What can he do really well which will help the performance of the organization?'

We Did It Ourselves

A manager's main task is to ensure that his men do a good job — that's when he gets his biggest kick. 'To lead people, walk behind them.' That's what wise old Lao-Tzu said many centuries ago. He

WE MADE THIS OURSELVES!

went on to say: 'People don't notice the existence of the best leaders. The next best, people honour and praise. The next, people fear, and the next, people hate. When the best leader's work is done, his people will say, 'We did it ourselves.'

This was true many hundreds of years ago when the Chinese built their Great Wall; it is equally true today for building our nuclear ships. The real leader does not throw his weight around. Yet somehow his people always seem to turn out better work compared to that of others.

The test of a good executive is to make ordinary people achieve uncommon performance. But this is only possible if the organization is properly managed. Good organization enables people to give off their best; or else they will spend a disproportionate amount of time merely patching up mistakes instead of making any real contribution.

2

Hierarchy

The word 'hierarchy' meant, originally, an organized priesthood in successive grades. Beneath the organization's chief executive, there are directors, managers, assistant managers and so on, with possible caste barriers between the executive and the supervisors; between the clerical and manual staff. In larger firms there tends to be a stronger sense of hierarchy; a priestly atmosphere in the boardroom; a feeling that the managing director's room is the holy of holies. Up to a point, this solemnity may serve a useful purpose, but there are dangers against which we have to guard. While the chief executive must make his presence felt, he must not allow the wage-earners to think of the company as an abstraction, as a vague entity by which they are employed. They must be made to realize that they *are* the company. This is difficult for them to grasp because the presence of a hierarchy is oppressive. Organizational hierarchy can be likened to the hierarchy of the Indian caste system where Brahmins are found at the top, and the 'untouchables' at the bottom. Rigid barriers separate one caste from the other. It is unwise, therefore, to draw too firm a line between those with a collar and tie and those without, and just as unwise to encourage class distinctions among the executives themselves. It is a human instinct to create these barriers, but it should be company policy to minimize rather than emphasize their significance. A common mistake is for the chief executive to have an executive assistant who stands between him and his senior executives. This power, if misused, can cause a lot of friction as it tends to undermine the authority of the supervisory staff. In any administrative machine, there are points which need oiling. If we neglect them, there will be over-heating causing a possible breakdown.

The authority has to be there but it should not be too obvious. It should not be over-burdened by protocol, ceremony and the clicking of heels. Some hint of rank is useful in that it may save embarrassment — as when the car park attendant shouts rudely at someone who turns out to be the chairman of the board — but we should not have too much of it. Should there be reserved parking space for each director and manager? One writer on organization has sugguested that anyone who is that important should arrive early in the morning to take his pick. That may be a little unfair, for the chief executive may have to attend another meeting first, but the point is well taken. Effective authority does not rest upon privileges but upon greater knowledge, dedication and energy. A man who is a ball of fire needs no status symbol, no bulging briefcase. He is a man whom other people naturally look up to for orders in an emergency. To be working under him is a source of pride in itself. A good leader can show that he is one without having to be specially or differently attired. As anyone can see, he is the boss.

One Sort of Change . . .

. . . that's what you have in a night club when girls take off their clothes. In management too, a time comes when a change just has to be made. Up to a certain point, an individual's skill is measured by his knowledge of his own particular field of specialization which may be finance, metallurgy, research, purchasing, personnel or accounts. But as he goes higher, there must be a change. This is not at all easy. You will be surprised at the number of chief executives who still fail to have an overall view of their organization. They are still blinded by their former field of specialization. They just can't get away from it.

28

It is a bad situation if a chief executive runs only his favourite department instead of the whole business. This prevents the department manager concerned from doing his own job properly because he would not be able to concentrate with the chief executive breathing down his neck. Moreover, the co-ordination and the running of the rest of the business also suffers.

The Company Is No Spectral Image

Why should people refer to 'the company' as if it were some sort of spectral image hovering in the background? We are always talking about the various things the company should do. But we never seem to realize that *we* also have a big responsibility in this. In the last analysis, it is only through our own efforts that the company can do the things it does. It is people like us who make up 'the company'. So it is pointless to talk about 'the company' as

if it were some separate being with whom we have no direct connection.

Boss is Boss . . .

. . . you might be a better man than your boss. That's all very well, but, if there is to be any sort of discipline, you must respect the authority of your boss. Any failure to do so must be brought home to the person straightaway.

Brahmins and Non-Brahmins

These used to be entirely distinct and separate categories. Much of such segregation can be found in the average organization, causing a lot of frustration.

You will be astonished at the amount of time and energy people spend on status symbols.

Reserved parking places, special quality stationery, use of company planes, separate lifts, separate dining halls, the size of offices, the type of furniture; all these distinctions give rise to time-wasting arguments. Tread very carefully. The days of the Brahmins and non-Brahmins are over and the fewer the distinctions you make, the better it will be for everybody.

Executive Assistant

Normally, there is no job for which he is actually responsible. But unless kept on a tight rein, he can do any amount of damage by causing confusion and making extra work. It is all too easy for him to come between the president and the senior line executives; just as it is easy for him to favour some individuals over others. He may even cause much frustration if he starts throwing his weight around. An executive assistant is like fire; properly under control, he can be very useful to the boss, but out of control, he can be disastrous.

Just Like That . . .

. . . if you criticize your supervisor in public you will destroy his goodwill and co-operation, just as surely as you will destroy a

machine with a sledge hammer. Whatever happens, never criticize your supervisor publicly. Do so if you must, but only when no one is around. And if you want to write him a nasty letter, mark it 'Personal and Strictly Confidential'. If you don't support your supervisor, his men will not respect him. Then, he becomes useless to you and everyone else.

Avoiding a Breakdown . . .

. . . that's what our supervisor is doing. He is always on the look out for things that might go wrong. He knows that if all the parts

of the machine are checked periodically and well in time, he will avoid breakdowns in the future. With human beings it is exactly the same. People need attention on a regular and systematic basis the way a machine needs periodic checking and lubrication. In this way, you keep them happy and avoid breakdowns in efficiency and morale.

In a car there are certain vital contact points. These must be checked periodically. In organizations, the vital contact points are the relationship between, say, a Managing Director and his senior officers, or between a supervisor and his men. These sensitive areas have to be periodically checked. If there is any heat or friction, you can be sure that something is out of gear.

Who Comes to Whom?

You will be amazed at the amount of heat generated by an apparently simple matter such as this: 'A' thinks that 'B' should come to him because he is higher up in the hierarchy, but 'B' thinks he is the man who is higher up. Such apparently trivial matters can cause any amount of tension. The good leader has a wonderful way of getting over this. He just doesn't bother about protocol. He goes right over and sees people in their own offices.

Not only does this give him a better idea of what is going on, but, more importantly, it gives an enormous boost to the ego of the person whom he visits. Moreover, it keeps him on his toes because he never knows when the boss may decide to drop in.

Nothing At All

You can't tell the difference between the colonels and the privates except by a small badge indicating their rank. They wear the same type of uniform. Their food is the same. Their colonels walk like the privates or cycle with them. They live on the food they carry and the game they shoot. No glamorous secretaries, no elaborate rations, no cars with waving flags, no motor-cycle cavalcades, no bands, no special helicopters. As a result, Ho Chi Minh's men performed a miracle.

What a lesson for all of us in our own ordinary day to day life! We normally find it difficult to resist the panoply and trappings of power and authority: the salutes, the limousines and the braided uniform. Perhaps, we would also do as well as Ho Chi Minh if we were to ease up a little on these things.

It's So Much Better . . .

. . . to have a boss who does not try to impress people with his authority and ability all the time. This is true of a boss who is confident of his own ability. He knows he is efficient and assumes that others will find out sooner or later. It's certainly far less strenuous working for a boss who does not constantly try to prove to you that he's the boss.

No Wonder He's Happy

It's the right atmosphere. This is a vague phrase you might say. True enough. But you can sense it immediately when you go somewhere which has it. Similarly, when the atmosphere is not right, you become aware of it at once.

Employees naturally like to work in an atmosphere which is comfortable, and that's what customers like too. The creation of the right atmosphere is not easy. Everyone has to play his part in it.

But the main emphasis and drive must come from the top. It is up to senior management to lay down standards of performance and behaviour which will induce a feeling of pride in every member of the organization; standards which everyone in the organization will try their utmost to achieve. If management is successful in inculcating this feeling of pride in its members, that important but undefinable thing which we call atmosphere would be developed.

One of the best ways of creating a good atmosphere is to let people in an organization do as much as possible themselves and to let the decisions be made at the lowest level possible. This is also the best way to train executives. And let them know that you're really interested in developing their talents. Let them take decisions, and make mistakes. Shift them around from one job to another. Expose them to different situations. Give people responsibility, and they will grow quickly, from boys into men, and some of the men into managers.

3

Delegation

A craftsman is skilled as in mending a clock or carving an ivory elephant. On a higher level the manager needs something different: the art of getting the work done through other people: as in organizing a clock factory or opening an ivory-carving workshop. The basic secret of managerial art is that of delegation. This means more than merely choosing the right man for each task; it means allowing him to do it in his own way. Power that is delegated is effectively transferred (as when Number One goes on holiday), and should not to be recalled unless something goes wrong. The man to whom power is transferred is thus made responsible for ensuring (in his own way) that success is achieved. The manager who cannot delegate will collapse from overwork, leaving a difficult situation for someone else. Big decisions must of course be taken by Number One, but the organization in which nobody else dares take a decision will not flourish for long. Each executive should be encouraged to plan ahead and sort out his own difficulties. The best men do not like to be treated as puppets. They like to be given the opportunity to show some initiative. This may result in an occasional error of judgement, but such errors are the price we must pay for developing the confidence of our subordinates. The worst mistake of all is to make oneself indispensable by having weak lieutenants.

To build up the efficiency of your staff, there are three basic rules. First, delegate authority properly and then leave them to get on with it. Second, make it a rule never to short-circuit your supervisors by giving orders other than through them. Third, you must never allow your supervisors to feel unsupported. All these are aspects of delegation. At the top level, there are two aspects of work. The more pressing of the two is the daily activities of the firm, the production and marketing, the delivery and cash transactions, the paying of wages and the keeping of accounts. The other, which is more important, is planning for the future, watching the market and studying the trend. It is essential to keep these two functions separate, providing for the second without neglecting the first. This is possible only with the man who delegates.

Just As There Is Craftsmanship . . .

. . . in making an ivory elephant, so there is craftsmanship in management. But the conditions must be favourable. An example

of an unfavourable situation is that of a supervisor in a highly centralized organization. He is completely tied down by rules and regulations and has very little scope for developing his own individuality. The only thing such a frustrated individual is likely to develop is ulcers.

On the other hand, a much luckier supervisor is one who works in a firm where authority and responsibility are decentralized. This gives the supervisor a feeling that he has a very definite say in the running of his department. And that's where management skill and craftsmanship come in. In an atmosphere like this he can use his ability to the fullest; he can see the results of his effort; he can be just as much a craftsman as the fellow who makes the elephant.

You Will Be Surprised . . .

. . . that many a boss are scared of selecting strong subordinates: people who are more capable or are as capable as himself. He's worried that if somebody smarter should turn up, he may be asked to retire prematurely. So he makes sure that no one with any initiative or enterprise comes into his section.

But he forgets that if he has weak and ineffectual subordinates, he will never be able to move up to a higher job himself because no one is available to take on his present job. And he'll always have far too much work to do because he hasn't trained people to take over some of his own load.

It's Obvious, Isn't It?

Anyone would collapse in his place. Just as intricate machinery needs the periodic attention of qualified engineers, so does the human body, which requires periodic check-ups by a doctor. But our boss says he doesn't believe in doctors and he is far too busy anyway. He also feels he has no time for holidays, or even for regular exercise. He seems to forget that it is not the time spent that is important, but the quality of his work. There's no question about it. A fit man will turn out work which is of far better quality in an hour than some one who's not as fit. Our boss

always works in a high state of tension. The net result is that he can't distinguish the important from the trivial. He makes mountains out of mole-hills.

He would in fact, be far more productive if he had learned to relax and played a bit of golf or tennis, or went for morning walks. Not only would his work be much better but he would also be a much easier man to get along with at home.

Why Should He Read It?

Mr X is a specialist. He is a senior man and is well paid. So why should the chief executive have to check his work? A good chief executive lets his subordinates know that he will unquestioningly accept what they do; that he will sign without looking. But he makes it entirely clear that the responsibility for what they have done is theirs.

Once an individual realizes that the responsibility lies with him, he will do his utmost to do everything right. But if he knows that the Big Boss is there to check what he has done, his sense of responsibility will diminish and he is bound to do that much less. The Boss is a wise man. By putting responsibility where it properly belongs, by delegating authority to the right subordinates, he makes sure that his evening briefcase will have very few papers.

Carrying It Too Far?

Some of us might think he is, but he's an experienced boss who knows what he is doing. He knows that the best way to develop a sense of responsibility in people is to let them do things on their own; to trust them and not look over their shoulders all the time. He knows that Mr X will do everything to demonstrate that he can run the show.

The Use of Time

The average executive has many datelines to meet, and unless he learns to manage his time well, he can be completely swamped with work. Consequently, his contribution to the organization will become insignificant. An executive must learn how to conserve his time. It is not simply a question of a course in fast reading, nor a rule limiting reports to one page or interviews to fifteen minutes. It goes much deeper than that.

Uninterrupted time is essential

For the type of work in which he is involved, an executive must have long stretches of uninterrupted time. Nothing worthwhile can be done in bits and pieces: for example, important decisions regarding personnel, their recruitment, placement and development cannot be taken in a hurry. For such matters, considerable time is required. Similarly, for the development of new products, the expansion of the factory, increase in production and the development of a strategy to get more customers, the executive needs time to plan.

But often it is these very same tasks which they do in dibs and dabs that bury them in a mass of relatively unimportant work. So it becomes difficult for them to do their real work well. If such important work is done in bits and pieces, it becomes a sheer waste of time because nothing worthwhile can be accomplished in this manner and the work and thinking already done has to be done all over again.

The question that should be always asked is 'What happens if a particular job is not done at all, or if a particular visit not made at all.' Some busy people spend a surprising amount of time on tasks which would never be missed in the first place if they were not done.

Delegation is not an entirely correct term

The most time-consuming tasks are those which a senior executive should not be doing. These tasks could easily be done by other officers in his organization but which, due to bad management, come to him for a decision. The word delegation is perhaps not an entirely correct word. It is a matter of organizing work and duties in such a manner that certain types of routine work do not come to the senior executive at all. Routine work should be handled by the lower levels right from the start. The most salient thought in the mind of an executive should be 'What am I contributing?', 'Am I contributing enough to deserve my pay?', 'Or am I doing work which a lower salaried person can do?'

People take up time

- Dealing with people takes up the bulk of an executive's time; but people can also waste a lot of his time unless he is careful. An important part of an executive's job is sometimes to settle down with his juniors and have a quiet heart-to-heart talk with them: about the organization itself, the contribution which they are making and their ideas for exploiting opportunities and developing the organization. Decisions about people are also important because no one ever fits exactly into a job. One has to make the best out of the choices one has — but all this takes time.

- The more people there are in an organization, inevitably, the more time will be spent on problems concerning people interacting with each other: their leave applications, their quarrels, etc. Unless an executive is watchful, he will find that a disproportionate amount of his time is taken up with the 'inside' details of the organization, rather than on the contribution which his organization has to make to the 'outside': to its customers, the improvement of its products, its future plans of growth and its interaction and relationships with other departments and organizations.

Meetings can use up time

- Meetings are great time wasters. Too many meetings are a sure sign of bad organization. It means that things are not working smoothly and meetings are necessary to straighten them out. Hours are sometimes spent in discussions even before the first draft emerges. Perhaps this could be done by someone else.

Often in the case of a big research establishment, much of the time of an important research director is spent making out a press report. This could be done just as effectively by someone lower down in the hierarchy who is not only less expensive but who can also, in all probability, write much better than the research director.

- Meetings involving a large number of people seldom solve anything and they certainly waste a lot of valuable time. The best meeting consists of just the two or three people directly involved. This not only saves a considerable amount of time but it also gets the job done much better. You will be surprised at the amount of time wasted by people who come to meetings just out of prestige and status because someone higher up in the hierarchy is also attending.

Example of Harry Hopkins

A significant example of time saving is shown in the person of Harry Hopkins, who was President Roosevelt's adviser during World War II. Harry Hopkins was a very sick man; he was dying. But he did enormously valuable work simply because he was too sick to attend to anything except to the core of a problem. He had no time or energy for anything but the basic essentials. Executives can learn a great deal from Harry Hopkins' example: he limited his efforts to dealing only with the essentials and this was the secret of his success.

Time cannot be stretched

- Time is inelastic. Everyone has exactly the same amount of it — you cannot have more than twenty-four hours in a day — and time lost can never be regained. To accomplish anything, time is required. One can get more money if one tries hard enough. One can also recruit more people. But one cannot rent, hire or buy more time: we all have just that much and no more.

- Very few executives analyse how they spend their time. There is a big difference between how they think their time is spent and the reality. In one case, a senior executive thought he devoted a quarter of his time to co-ordinating work with his senior officers, a quarter on community activities, a quarter on research and development and the last quarter on liaising with his biggest customers. However, on a detailed examination of his work, it was found that the bulk of his time was spent in chasing up orders of some of his customers who happened to be known personally to him. He never had more than ten minutes at a stretch for any one single job without an interruption, with the result that he was really doing the work of a chaser and not the job for which he was paid: the tasks on which he thought he was spending the bulk of his time but which in fact he was not doing at all. One of the first things a leader who wishes to be more effective has to learn to do is to analyse his time and to know how it actually goes.

Use of the telephone

The telephone can be a real time waster. It can interrupt a line of thought or an important decision which is in the process of being thought out. The telephone should not be allowed to do this because it often means that the whole process of thinking and work has to be started all over again. A few carefully worded instructions to your secretary or telephone operator can save an enormous amount of time by avoiding interruptions. Such interruptions should therefore be cut down except where they are absolutely unavoidable. After all, there is hardly any matter that cannot wait for at least 60 minutes. And these 60 minutes of uninterrupted time mean so much to an executive.

Travelling can waste time

Travelling can also be a waste of time. Seldom are there tasks which cannot be done equally well on the telephone or by someone lower down in the hierarchy, who would have more time, energy and inclination to travel and who would be an equally good substitute in most cases if he is properly briefed.

Why executives take work home

The reason why working at home in the evenings is so popular with many executives is that they do not have the capacity for organizing and managing their time during the working day. So they are compelled to work in the evenings. But they must try to avoid this because their overall efficiency will eventually be reduced. However, reading general articles and books which are relevant to their jobs is something that can be profitably done in the evenings. This will not only enable them to update their knowledge, but will give them a better approach towards their tasks.

He Simply Must Have Time

It is not fair to expect someone who is continually tied up in the rush and bustle of day-to-day activities to be able to think out and plan clearly an organization's long term objectives. The chief executive takes the responsibility for an organization and for its future. If he is to achieve his aim, he simply must keep himself free from day-to-day problems. He must delegate. His main task lies in thinking ahead and working out plans for the future. He must put it all in the right perspective and ensure that he is abreast of the latest thinking. So it is vital that he is not all the time tied up with everyday activities.

People Don't Like It . . .

. . . they don't like being treated like puppets who can be played around with. They don't like the supervisor to do all the thinking

and planning himself. They like to participate. They like to feel that they too have a hand in doing a job. No one likes to be manipulated like a puppet. It just won't get you results.

What Do You Expect . . .

. . . how can anyone work under these circumstances? Even the best of supervisors will be completely frustrated. Once somebody is in the saddle, you must support him; otherwise it is simply not reasonable to expect him to produce good results.

It Is Fatal

If you put a man in charge of a group of people, work through him and not around him. Don't undermine his authority by giving direct orders; this is the fastest way of lowering discipline and morale.

What Do You Prefer?

You would think that many of the executives and managers would prefer to have complete solutions given to them for their approval in order to save work, worry and trouble. But you will be surprised at the number of bosses who do not like their men to give them solutions. They insist on making all the decisions themselves. So everyone brings them problems — problems which the executive has to work out on his own. The result is that he gets completely snowed under with infructuous work; he has no time to do anything constructive. A good executive should never allow his people to bring him problems — he should insist that they come up with definite recommendations.

Lack of Initiative

Often the fault is really the boss's. He kills initiative without realizing that he has done so. Some bosses hate allowing people to share responsibility. They keep all important matters tightly in their own hands. Some bosses consider subordinates' suggestions as an insult to their own ability and judgement. If someone takes the initiative and makes a blunder, blame is heaped on him. Can you wonder then, that people normally hate sticking their necks out and taking the initiative?

4

Management by Objectives

The traditional concept of management has always been that of the boss who directs and controls. However, over the last few years, there has been a change in emphasis: the thinking now is that the unit or section manager in an organization should be directed not so much by his boss but rather by the tasks that have to be done. The managers of the various units or sub-units or sections of an organization should know about the objectives of their units. They should also know how the objectives of their unit fit in with the objectives of the organization as a whole. The

manager of each unit or sub-unit must not only actively participate in setting these objectives but must also take responsibility for them. A manager must know what is expected of him and what criteria will be used to measure him against. Through management by objectives there is a meeting of minds within the entire organization. Each unit and each sub-unit is fully conversant with its own objectives, the needs and objectives of the other units and the objectives of the organization as a whole. Management by objectives makes it possible for a manager to control his own performance and that of his subordinates, since he himself has actively participated, given his agreement and assumed responsibility for the objectives of his unit. Once the objectives are fixed, the manager should be allowed to get on with the job of achieving them in any manner he thinks best. And he should be left to do so.

The advantage of this approach is, firstly, that it frees the senior executive from a great deal of detailed supervisory work and, secondly, the work becomes much more interesting and worthwhile for the section manager who is doing it. This, very simply put, is the essence of management by objectives.

Management by Objectives Helps Teamwork

Under the philosophy of management by objectives, an individual manager acts not because somebody orders him to do so but because he himself decides what he has to perform. He acts, in other words, as a free man: it's virtually management by self-control. This applies to every manager whatever his level and functions, and to any type of business enterprise which he might be working in, whether large or small. It ensures that things get done by making sure that the objectives of a section are also the personal goals of the individual manager. This means that the progress of a unit or a department of an organization is directly linked up with the progress of its various section managers: what greater incentive could there be for a manager?

For any organization to work effectively, it is necessary that

every task of every unit in that organization be directed towards this: each individual manager must know and understand the overall aims of the organization and what is required from his own particular unit to achieve those aims. This is surely the best way of getting participation from everyone and also first-class teamwork.

Factors That Cause Disintegration

What is not fully realized is that there are always factors in an organization which tend to pull it apart. One factor would be the specialization of managers. A manager in charge of a specialized function may be so anxious and keen about his own specialized function that he concentrates on this alone, often to the detriment of the organization as a whole. There is also the very ambitious manager of a unit. His aim is to show up the performance of his own unit, irrespective of the overall objectives of the organization. Other such disintegrating factors are dissatisfaction, company politics, empire building and so on.

By far, the most effective manner in which these disintegrating factors can be overcome is to run the organization on the principle of management by objectives. The objectives for each section should be clearly spelt out and individual managers should be entirely clear in their minds as to what the overall objectives of the organization are and how the objectives of their own particular unit meshes in with them. Right from the start, the emphasis should be on teamwork and team spirit. If you can achieve this atmosphere, you will be armed with an effective counter-weapon to arrest the disintegrating trends which are innate in every organization.

Management by Objectives Is Specially Important for Service Sections

For the service industry and highly specialized groups such as

58

computer programmers — and the importance of this group has grown enormously over the last 15 years — it may not always be possible to relate their work directly to business objectives and business results. Unless this is done, however, they are likely to direct their work away from business objectives and results and work on problems which they find interesting. In the service industry as well as in certain organizations, one comes across empire building and clannish tendencies. And that is why management by objectives is especially important to the service industry. The emphasis must always be towards the main goals of the organization and on teamwork. If there is sufficient emphasis on this and if the principles of management by objectives are used, the separatist and clannish tendencies that are inherent in the service industry can be overcome and they will all work towards the common goal.

Management by Drives

Where you do not have management by objectives, you sometimes have management by crises and drives. This puts all the emphasis on one phase of the job to the detriment of everything else. A sales drive, a drive to cut inventory or to save staff are examples. The result is that people either neglect their jobs to get on with the current drive or they organize themselves for collective sabotage of the drive in order to get their own work done. In fact, management by drives indicates that management does not think; that the company does not know what to expect of its managers; and that not knowing how to direct, misleads.

Helps in the Development of Managers

When you have a philosophy of management by objectives and decentralization, it also means that the various levels of management are reduced and this gives an opportunity to aspiring young men to use their abilities and skills far earlier than in a centralized organization. Too many steps in the hierarchy between the lowest and highest tend to make junior executives disheartened and despondent simply because it will take them a long time before they reach a senior position, in the charge of responsible work. Organizationally, the Catholic Church is thought to be among the best in the world. It has only one level of management between the parish priest and the Pope, and that is the Bishop.

The best way of training an executive is to give him an actual job to do and make him responsible for it. Working as a lieutenant or assistant does not adequately prepare a person for the task of making his own decisions under pressure. In fact, there are many cases where trusted and effective lieutenants have collapsed when they were left on their own. The best training is on the job.

Another important by-product of putting a trainee executive into a job and making him responsible for it as early as possible is that this enables management to test the quality and capabilities of that executive. But the executive should be junior enough so that, if he fails, he can be removed and put into a position where his capabilities can be better utilized. However, if a senior man such as a president or vice-president falls down on a job, it is difficult to remove him. In publicly owned corporations where ownership is completely dispersed, it is almost impossible. An organization sometimes gets stuck with a President who is incompetent: nothing short of providence or coronary thrombosis can get rid of him.

Treatment of Audit and Control Reports

Trust is basic in management by objectives and this is illustrated in the manner in which reports and audit staff are used. In many well-managed organizations the reports of the auditors and control information do not go to the bosses at headquarters at all, but are given direct to the individual managers themselves. This system builds up the confidence and self-esteem of the individual managers and you can be certain that when control reports come to them direct, and not to the higher-ups, they will try their hardest to put right all the deficiencies noted in such reports. And look at the amount of unnecessary correspondence this saves. In any other system the individual manager would have to give long explanations on the audit report and control statements to the central office instead of getting on with the job straightaway and putting right the blemishes noted in such reports.

Reports and other such control documents should be cut down to the minimum: to try to control everything is to control nothing. Only those reports which are of real use to the manager to help him in his performance should be made out. All others should be cut out. Too many reports sometimes result in a manager's performance being judged by the quality of his reports rather than by his actual performance.

Among the great advantages of management by objectives and self-control is that it makes it possible for a manager to control his own performance. This motivates him to give off his best as against working just to get by. Management by objectives is a far more effective way of getting things done compared to management by domination with a boss breathing down your neck all the time.

5

Communicate and
Co-ordinate

Communication requires more imagination than many people imagine or, indeed, possess. We begin as children, with the assumption that what we know is also known to everyone else. Directing a complete stranger, the helpful villager will begin by saying 'Well you know where Mr Martin's cottage was before it was burnt down? Turn after passing that and . . .' Today, the phrase which few people can exclude from their conversation is 'You know,' suggesting that the person addressed already knows what he is about to be told. But he does not know and it would be pointless in telling him if he did. Our central difficulty in communication is to decide, by an effort of imagination, the extent of other people's knowledge or ignorance. Having solved that problem, our next task is to give them just the right amount of information, to be delivered in an unambiguous manner. It is the study of a lifetime to convey even the simplest thought with precision and brevity. You end, it is true, with the obvious precaution of asking 'Is that clear?' but you would be wrong to regard silence as proof of comprehension. On the one hand, your message is clear to those who have misunderstood it. On the other hand, it is meaningless to those who are too shy to admit their confusion. It is not always a case of stupidity. The trouble can begin with a doubt in the mind of the man who issues the directive or makes the announcement. If the trumpet sounds an uncertain note, who shall prepare himself for battle?

Remember, not everyone wants to communicate. Some people prefer mystery, humiliating their subordinates by telling them only part of what they need to know. This leads to mistakes and provides them the opportunity to blame their subordinates for stupidity and ignorance. A favourite trick with the mystery men is to turn away before completing what they have to announce, their last words being lost as they walk off. This prevents anyone asking them to repeat the message. Another trick is to mumble the key word indistinctly and, when asked for clarification, mumble the same word in exactly the same tone instead of choosing a different phrase to convey the same meaning. The object of this behaviour is to give the mystery man a sense of superiority. He knows more than he chooses to reveal and people who are still in the dark must be inattentive, half-witted or deaf. This is a device which is all too familiar in television drama. The play fades out without reaching any sort of conclusion thus saving the dramatist the trouble of writing the final scene. Yet many people say 'How interesting!' in order to give the impression of intelligence. Nobody, in fact, has a clue as to what the story is about and in all probability, the author knows as little as anyone else. There is little chance of good communication when there are people around whose preference is for mystery. There is already too much muddle in the world without our deliberately making it worse.

Take a firm, for instance, which undertook two projects, A and B. The first, A, is quickly successful and the file dealing with it remains slim and neat. The second, B, runs into trouble and the file in this case is a foot thick and spilling over. It often transpires that the first enclosure on file A was precise and lucid, making it crystal clear what had to be done, but that the original document on file B was vague and ambiguous, being the root cause of all the subsequent confusion. Where the originator of the scheme is vague, we may suppose that others who try to implement the idea will be vaguer still. Most human disasters can be traced back to an early failure to decide what exactly we are trying to do. Remember, however, that you can communicate effectively in other ways. One way is by example. By showing interest in any activity, Number One can indicate that he thinks it important. His views can also be gauged from his casual conversation, which may seem less casual in retrospect than it seemed at the time. He can sometimes teach more by his example than he can on paper. For much that is good or bad in the general atmosphere, he is, at least indirectly, responsible. If the girl on the switchboard is helpful, cheerful and patient, she may have learnt it from him; and she is (almost needless to say) one of the most important people in the whole factory. If the Managing Director cannot find a nice girl for that key position, it is most unlikely that he can find anything else. Good public relations begins from there.

Communication established, the next need is for co-ordination which is a problem, above all, for Number One. It is his task to make people work together as a team. He must show that the success of the organization depends upon the success of each department. He must remember that failure to consult somebody can cause endless trouble. He must remember that while people should not be over-supervised, they do like to know what is happening. Attempts to influence them should be soft-pedalled except in time of crisis but they should be given information regularly and in some detail. Remember that what they are not told they will probably invent. Rumours will be current in any case — this is unavoidable — but they will be less harmful if the facts are readily available to everyone.

He's Obviously Confused . . .

. . . so what he types is not at all clear to anyone. In the same way, a print can never be any clearer than the negative. So an executive cannot convey his ideas convincingly to his subordinates unless these ideas have crystallized clearly in his own mind.

You'll be surprised, but one of the main reasons for poor communication is that people themselves are not at all clear in their own minds about what they want to communicate.

Fatal . . .

. . . 'I thought he meant that', 'I did not realize this is what he wanted.' These are all phrases to be dreaded — but how often

65

we hear them. Misunderstandings, misunderstandings and yet more misunderstandings. It is because people do not bother to double check. They fail to realize that it is possible to get hold of the wrong end of the stick. It happens again and again. Check with somebody else. Be certain you understand.

It Follows, Doesn't It?

If the boss is interested in flowers, his men will go all out to see

that the gardens of the factory are well-kept. People are always trying to anticipate what the bosses are going to inspect. Then they make an effort to ensure that that particular item will be in order. So if the boss is interested in personnel matters, you can be sure that his supervisors will spend time ensuring that their personnel policies are properly worked out. And so it goes on. The boss should try to become interested in as many aspects of the work as he possibly can. In this way, he will keep his men constantly on their toes.

He's Always Talking

Very often good bosses have this scoffing remark thrown at them. And people go on to say, 'When does he ever get any work done?' But this is where they are entirely wrong. Because talking to people, either individually or together, is precisely what managers

should be doing. How else can they communicate? How else can they make sure that what they want done has been properly understood right down the line? How else can they make people feel that they are part of a team? He tells them how they are getting on, their strong points and their weaknesses. When a manager is talking to his people, he is doing his real job. Writing letters, dictating, meeting VIPs are not nearly as important.

Even the World's Best . . .

. . . advertising agency cannot give you effective public relations if your organization is a poor one. No matter how much re-touching it does, it won't help. Public relations can only reflect what you actually are.

The way your telephone operators answer the phone, the tone of your letters, the quality of letter paper, the way your men talk and behave, the products you make — all these are really your most effective public relations.

Worth a Thousand Words . . .

. . . that's what the ancient Chinese used to say of a picture. And how very true it is. It's so much easier to understand things and to explain things, if they are accompanied by photographs or drawings. Bill and his friends are taking it easy — our supervisor has clear proof. Bill certainly won't be able to talk himself out of this.

Communication Upwards Is More Important Than Communication Downwards

The important thing about communication is that more emphasis should be laid on it going upwards rather than downwards. An executive should ask his men periodically what he should expect from them; how he should hold them accountable and what is the best use he can make of their knowledge and ability. It is surprising how seldom people ask their subordinates these questions. But if they do, the results can be most rewarding in that better communication would be attained.

Some well-managed organizations have a managers' half-yearly letter to the chief executive, where the various managers outline their own duties and also note what they require in the form of help from the chief executive. This periodical report has been found to be most useful in contributing to better communication and understanding.

Good managers spend far more time on upward communication than on downward communication. They do not talk to their men about their own problems, but they know how to make their subordinates talk about theirs. They spend a great deal of their time carefully going through the half-yearly letter where each subordinate sets down the objectives of his job, his plans and what his superior does to help or hamper him. The result of all this is that the management does not have to worry much about its downward communication: this becomes a natural and effortless by-product of any organization which has good upward communication. And it makes all the difference if everyone knows what is going on.

An accountant brings out masses of figures but he seldom asks the operating personnel, for whom these figures are intended, in what form they would like to have the figures presented. The result is that little use is made of the figures; and the personnel receiving the figures have to work them out by themselves at the cost of a lot of trouble and effort which could have been entirely avoided if there was better communication between the accounts and operations departments.

When Management Tries to Convey Information

Top management does a considerable amount of hard thinking in working out its objectives. It takes the advice of everyone and, after much thought and discussion, it decides on the action that should be taken.

The next level of management receives the result of all this hard work and thinking in, say, three or four meetings. Then it goes to the next level, and the next level and so on. But when it finally gets to the first-line supervisors, they only receive either a few minutes' explanation or a brief note. The result is that the top management's original concepts become less and less clear as they filter down through the various levels of management. And this happens very frequently.

This brings out the important difference between information and communication. Throughout the ages, the problem has been to get communication. This is because when information has to be handled and transmitted by people, it is always distorted by communication: that is, by opinion, impression, bias and so on. That's why it is important to try to ensure that information doesn't get garbled, and that people at all levels know what's cooking and what the policy is.

Learning Poetry and Communication

A manager only becomes effective if his communication is good. After all, his main job is to deal with people, to get them to do what is required, and also to interpret the orders of his own superiors. So an effective manager must be skilled in getting his thinking across to other people and he must also be able to find out what other people are after. You may be surprised to read this, but learning poetry and writing essays are also good training in management because they teach the manager the value of words and this, in turn, helps him to communicate.

Many a Good Idea . . .

. . . have come to naught because somebody who ought to have been consulted was not. Once a person's pride is hurt, it is very difficult to subsequently gain his co-operation.

71

Why Are They So Glum?

It's because they are being over-supervised. It is ruining their
morale and killing their job interest. If you give someone a job, let
him do it his way. Over-supervising can be frustrating. Delegating

responsibility and respecting it is one of the best ways of building up morale and increasing interest in the work.

Not a Hit-and-Miss Business

It is one of the tasks of management to provide conditions which make it easier for its staff to work in.

Its men should know that management is concerned and interested in them and is anxious that they make real progress.

They should be told what they have to do, what authority they have and who their boss is: the person to whom they can go when they want help and who dresses them down when they go off the rails.

They should be told periodically how they are getting on: their good points and bad ones.

The rules should be fair and should apply to all. People do not mind working hard — but when they hear of discrimination their blood pressure shoots up.

He's Soft-Pedalling.

No wonder, there is love in her thoughts. In day-to-day life too, we should learn to soft-pedal our opinions. Play it cool. 'Maybe I'm wrong', 'Isn't it possible?', 'One way of looking at it is' — these phrases are not double talk. This is how you will get your ideas accepted. You'll get people to listen to you.

People Like to Know . . .

. . . they are interested in everything about the company where they work — wages, prices, promotions, profits, new machinery, job changes. And they will insist on knowing. So give them all the information you can. In this way, there is less chance of their being confused by false rumours and speculation. Keep them informed all the time. It makes a big difference.

6

Organization

Throughout history, most people have faced problems of organization. There are too many people pestering Number One. The supervisor feels that he is being crushed between the management and the trade union. The departments are separated from each other by wooden partitions or, just as effectively, by the use of technical jargon. The work gets done but at an appalling cost. It is somehow finished but not in time. Even when delivered, nobody knows how to sell the product. Even when sold there is a failure in the supply of spare parts. Behind much of this confusion lies a common belief that the factory exists to provide employment, and that the client exists to keep the factory in business. We would do better to realize that the product is made to satisfy the customer and that the factory exists to supply the product.

Organization is very important, but it leads to a further problem which may be even more important: the right deployment of the people you have. The organization chart serves to show how the system is supposed to work, but nothing is achieved until the spaces on the chart are filled with actual names of actual people. It is apparent that people are no more uniform in ability or skill than they are in height and weight. Each is an individual and the manager's task is to place him where he will at once be useful and content. Each may have a special merit, as in being strong or honest, intelligent or loyal. But even his failings and handicaps may be made to serve a purpose. The one-legged veteran may be a good lift attendant. The obsessively tidy man may be a good filing clerk. A cheerful chatterbox might do well in the canteen and someone universally disliked could make an ideal night watchman. The manager who complains about the people he has to employ should realize that they are probably neither any worse nor better than any other work-force. It is his task to teach them and deploy them. Being people, they will present problems, but what of that? These are the problems he is paid to solve; and if there were no problems the manager would not even be needed.

The Number of People Who Report Directly to the Boss

You will be surprised how much tears are shed and how much nervous energy is expended by people who want to report directly to the big boss himself. Undoubtedly, they feel this gives them prestige and glamour. But this must be resisted at all cost.

In an organization, to be clear as to who is responsible to whom is basic knowledge. In the centralized type of organization, where a number of people report directly to the boss and where he gives them day-to-day directions, it is not possible for one boss to supervise more than a small number of people, especially in cases where these people have to work with each other and report to one manager. A greater number would only lead to confusion. He should not normally have more than, say, ten people directly responsible to him. This, in technical jargon, is called the 'span of control'.

In an organization based on the philosophy of management by objectives, a manager is not controlled in his day-to-day work by a boss who tells him what to do and who makes sure he does it. Here, a boss can have many more persons under him simply because he is not concerned with the detailed supervisory work of a unit, but only with the end results. This is called the 'span of managerial responsibility'.

Under the 'span of managerial responsibility', a boss may have fifty or even a hundred persons under him as contrasted with the

'span of control' described above, which extends to only about ten persons. Where good practice would counsel against stretching the 'span of control' too far, a manager under the 'span of managerial responsibility' should always have managerial responsibility for a few more men than he can really take care of. Otherwise, the tendency is for him to over-supervise them or to take over their jobs or, at least, to breathe down their necks.

At Least a Thousand People . . .

. . . in different parts of the world — New York, Bombay, Hong Kong, etc. — are handling problems identical to yours. Some are doing it better and some worse. Try to find out about the people who are handling your type of problems better. Get to learn what

they are doing and then improve on it. Get to know all the better ways of handling your own problems.

Squeezed between Workmen and Management . . .

. . . the foreman and other such middle level supervisors often face such situations. A lot of attention has been given to the cause of workmen; their conditions and their rights. Managers, too, have attracted plenty of attention. They have good perquisites and high salaries. But the middle level supervisor or foreman is frequently left out. He's rarely given proper training in basic management. In fact, he is too often forgotten.

Wooden Partitions . . .

. . . are not the only things that separate departments. Nowadays, separate sections in an organization use a very special language which only their own members can understand. The result is that communication between one section and another becomes completely clogged. For example, the accountant has his own language, which is difficult for an outsider to follow with the result that many of his reports, on which so much effort and money have been spent, do not really serve the purpose for which they were written. There is a growing complaint that lawyers, engineers, marketing men, personnel directors and sales managers are also using language which is understood only in their own departments. Very often, executives find it impossible to understand reports unless someone from the department concerned is

standing right by them to clarify. These tendencies must be resisted. Each section should stress the importance of using simple, non-technical language which can be understood by all.

Most People Can Get a Job Done . . .

. . . but at what cost? Having a hundred men and two excavators to dig a small hole is obviously extravagant. Surely the important thing to remember is the cost at which a job can be performed. If a

job is done with only two men where four men previously did it, then this is something one can be proud of. That's cost consciousness for you.

Too Much in too Little

In the fashion world this happens quite often. But you'll be surprised how often this happens in normal day-to-day life as well. Take people for instance. Too many people without enough work can do a lot of damage. It's the man without work who is the worst grouser and the worst trouble-maker. Take office space. If there is too much, it will be filled up in no time. Even if people do not want the space, they will be restless until they see it completely occupied. Take money. A tight budget makes a man much more inventive. People work best when they are under pressure. They'll raise hell to start with, but under pressure they simplify. They produce more and at lower cost.

Maybe We're Exaggerating . . .

. . . but it is certainly on the right lines. It is one thing to have a first-class product superbly manufactured. But it is equally important to ensure that first-class service goes with it.

It happens again and again. Poor salesmanship and weak after-sales service can ruin everything. A first class product can be left unsold whilst products which are not as good have record sales because they are being properly sold and serviced.

If the customer doesn't get good service or a good product everyone is going to pay the penalty. Squabbles between departments and differences between workers and management do not matter. The customer must surely always come first. Private differences may be settled later. If the customer doesn't buy, everyone's sunk.

Missed the Boat

This sort of thing happens often in ordinary life. People find any number of reasons to leave work unfinished: that they did not

have the necessary authority; that there was too much red-tape, and so on. However, even when there are a lot of restrictions on his authority, the good man will press on. And even if he does make a decision that he is not entitled to make, his superiors will probably support him. He is the sort of man who will see the work completed no matter what. He certainly won't miss the boat.

The Non-conformist

. . . is the man who lacks the capacity or the inclination to work with others. There are three alternatives in dealing with him. You can try to force him to conform by continual reprimand; or you can sack him; or else you can find a task to suit him: one which does not involve him with other people. He might be a good research chemist, a good metallurgist, or a man with first-class ideas. Don't be inflexible. These qualities of his may be useful. There's often room in an organization for the non-conformist if you know where to place him.

Striding Along

True enough. There are a number of things you have to take in your stride if you are to keep away from ulcers and tranquillizers. People, for example, are a varied lot: kind, perhaps, or mean, or unforgiving, or lazy. Their backgrounds vary, their vocations differ, their motivation, their clothes, ideas and thinking processes all follow different patterns. This is what a good executive should realize. There is no point in complaining. He must know that he just cannot have perfect individuals. He must do the best with what he has. This is what he is paid for. He must tackle problems one by one as they come and take it all in his stride — and keep smiling.

7
The Structure of Organization

Centralized Type of Organization

There is the centralized or functional type of organization, with separate sections or functions such as manufacturing, purchasing,

stores, accounting, finance, engineering, research and development and so on. These sections, with their managers, all report directly to the chief executive or the managing director. The centralized type of organization, however, starts becoming unwieldy as organizations grow in size, making it difficult to exercise proper control.

Federal Decentralization

A big change occurred in the structure of large organizations after the end of the First World War. Since then, the trend has been away from the centralized type of organization described above and towards what might be called 'federal decentralization'. Under a system of federal decentralization, the various units or sections in the organization are run as if they are separate autonomous businesses. For this type of management structure, control by top management is normally limited only to subjects such as finance, pricing and other such as these high level policy matters. This method of management has been adopted and fully developed by organizations such as Ford, Chrysler, General Motors (they had it from 1923), General Electric, Westinghouse, the major chemical companies, the oil companies and insurance companies. The main reasons for the emergence of this trend as the dominant structural principle of large businesses are as follows.

Advantages of Decentralization

- Decentralization means that the vision and effort of individual managers are fixed directly on business results.

- Under the old system of organization, where everything was centralized under one chief executive, unprofitable lines were carried on the back of profitable ones. There was concentration on products that were familiar and easy to handle, rather than on matters that were new and upcoming. Since everything was treated together and in lump sum total figures, many unprofitable lines of a business tended to stay hidden under the rug of 'total overhead costs' or in the 'total sales figures'.

- Under the system of decentralization where each individual manager is responsible for his organization and for his profit, he is compelled, in his own interest, to give up useless practices and uneconomical lines of manufacture. He has a personal interest in seeing that wasteful overheads do not creep in.

- The greatest strength of the decentralization principle, which often goes hand in hand with the principle of management by objectives, is with regards to management development. Of all the known principles of organization, this is the best way to prepare and test people for top management responsibilities, and at an early age. Under a system of decentralization and management by objectives, a manager reaches a position where he runs his own organization at a much earlier stage in his career than in any other system and this is excellent training for a future senior manager.

Decentralization and the Role of Top Management

Decentralization is a somewhat misleading term. One of the main purposes of decentralization is to strengthen top management and enable it to do its own work rather than be forced to supervise, co-ordinate and prop up the work of the various operating departments. It enables top management to concentrate on direction, strategy, objectives and making decisions for the future. Decentralization certainly does not mean a weakened top management. The type of decisions are reserved for top management are whether to abandon a business or go in for a new one. In some organizations, pricing decisions are in the hands of top management so that they can control the competition between the major units of their industry. In certain other organizations, top

management decides what kinds of goods to manufacture. The allocation of the key resource of finance is also usually in the hands of top management. The appointment of senior persons and their shifting around from one division to another is also a top management preserve.

New Type of Enterprise Necessitates New Organizational Structures

There has been a big change in organizations over the last fifteen years. The General Motors type of organization which has basically one product, vehicles; one language, English; and one country, the USA, is fast changing. The world, over the last fifteen years, is facing the challenge of organizing large multinational, non-manufacturing institutions and businesses such as world-wide transportation and customer service companies; and non-business service institutions such as hospitals, universities and government agencies. All these are now playing an increasingly greater part in present-day organized activity. These 'non-manufacturing' institutions are now increasingly becoming the true centre of gravity of any developed economy; their growth rate over the past fifteen years has been far greater, proportionately, than that of manufacturing units. They employ the greatest number of people and they both contribute to and make up most of the gross national product. Many of the relatively new businesses of today are multi-product, multi-technology and multinational.

The General Motors' pattern of federal decentralization cannot be applied to the big 'material' process businesses such as steel, aluminium, copper and glass; nor for railroads and airlines. These businesses are far too big to be controlled centrally and yet they are incapable of being genuinely decentralized because they cannot be divided into separate 'profit and loss' business units.

The kind of business and institution to be organized today is an enormously different type of beast from that of twenty years ago. These new businesses do not fit into the traditional organizational concepts, as many of these businesses and institutions are incapable of being genuinely decentralized and at the same time, they are too big to be managed centrally.

The problem today is the best structure of organization for these relatively new types of enterprise that have come up over the last few years.

There has clearly been a lot of thinking on this matter as can be seen from the continuous and far-reaching re-organizations which so many of these companies are having — sometimes almost on a yearly basis. There are many cases where substantial and even massive organizational surgery is being applied in order to take care of minor procedural problems. Sometimes executives are so caught up with re-organization that they neglect to think about the organization's objectives, strategies and priorities. The wrong structure of organization is a guarantee for bad performance and it produces friction and frustration.

Simulated Decentralization

As the new types of business and institution, which we have described in the previous paragraph, are too big to remain organized in one centralized unit and as some of them, especially the material process industries, are also too integrated to be able to be genuinely decentralized, we must think out a different type of organizational structure for them. For these types of organization, a system of 'simulated decentralization' is often the answer. Simulated decentralization sounds very complicated, but what it really means is that for an organization which cannot be divided into separate profit and loss business units, a compromise is made and this is how it is done: each section or unit of such an organization is given an arbitrary selling or transfer price for what it produces. This transfer price must necessarily be arbitrary as there is no 'market price' or, in other words, no price available for these items as they·are usually 'intermediate' items and in various stages of manufacture. The prices for these intermediate-stage items are necessarily fictitious. But under the circumstances, there is no better alternative and so these fictitious prices must be treated as if they are correct. By giving such fictitious prices, it is possible to make separate profit and loss centres for all types of business and, in this manner, the decentralized system of organization can be operated. For all its difficulties and defects, the system of simulated decentralized system of organization can be operated. For all its difficulties and defects, the system of simulated decentralization is probably the fastest growing organization design around these days. It is the only one that fits, albeit poorly, the computer, chemical, pharmaceutical, glass, steel and aluminium industries as well as the big banks. It is also the one design principle that is suited for universities, hospitals or government agencies. We must emphasize that, at best, it is a compromise: working out fictitious transfer prices is obviously subject to all sorts of pressures and prejudices. There is no question that the traditional principles of federal decentralization or the centralized system of organization should be used wherever possible. They are infinitely easier to work and involve no controversial and artificial policies of fictitious transfer prices.

Service or Functional Staff and Their Empires

What sometimes happens in a large organization is that service functions such as engineering, finance, purchasing, personnel management, material procurement and accounts, are under senior function executives at headquarters, who administer and control the service functions of individual units or sections throughout the organization. So the situation arises where the managers of individual sections of an organization are responsible for production alone, and all their service functions such as finance, material procurement, accounts, purchases and personnel are controlled by section heads who are responsible, not to them, but to their respective functional service chiefs at headquarters who in turn are often powerful members of top management. This type of organization has never worked satisfactorily in practice. The individual managers certainly need the

help of these functional specialists; but these specialists tend to concentrate on their own special functions rather than give help and advice to the managers.

In fact, sometimes instead of serving the manager who is responsible for production, the service or functional staff end up becoming his masters. They tend to push their own speciality, as if it were an end in itself and they are even inclined to undermine the manager's responsibility and authority. In actual practice, a manager's performance is often impeded by these entirely independent functional services and there is often friction and tension between these functional services and the managers.

Wherever possible, this type of system, which is still prevalent, should be avoided. The staff of the functional services should be an integral part of the unit to which they render functional service and should be responsible to, and directly controlled by, the manager who is responsible for production or for providing a service.

In order to ensure that the service chiefs at headquarters assist management and do not create empires of their own, the General

Electric Company insisted that a considerable amount of time of their functional service heads be spent as members of the chief executive team in order to ensure that their work keeps in line with the main objectives of the company; rather than let them create separate little empires.

Ideally, the service staff at the central office or headquarters should consist of a small handful of people. This is vastly preferable to the present system, where the importance of service staff and their contribution tend to be measured by the size of the payroll of their staff. Service chiefs should have no authority — line, functional or advisory — over operating managers. They should never be allowed to hold power over promotion of operating management: for whosoever controls a man's promotion, controls the man.

Organization Structures Should Be Tailor-made

We have spoken about the centralized and decentralized structures of organization. We have also discussed simulated decentralization. The important thing to remember, however, is that an organization structure must be tailor-made for each type of business or institution. There is no ideal standardized type of organization structure that can be imposed on a living business or institution. There may well be a position where the same business or institution can have three or more different types of organization structures in various areas of the same business organization. Some areas in the business may be suited for the centralized structure of management, other areas can be conveniently decentralized; and for other areas, one may have to adopt a system of simulated decentralization.

For structuring an organization, it is essential to adopt a pragmatic approach and to work out an organization structure most suited to the needs of a particular type of organization.

94

8

Promotion

When at or near the top, you will be concerned with the promotion of those who seem to deserve it. There is no more important task and you will do well to give it a lot of thought. There are, to begin with, some obvious mistakes to avoid. Never promise anyone a future vacancy, for the rumour of it will go round. A, to whom you have made the promise, will cease to bother, thinking his future secure; while B and C will equally cease to bother, thinking that they have been passed over. Avoid the least hint of nepotism. In the 'family firm' where only the founder's descendants are eligible for the top post, the abler executives see that they have no future and go elsewhere. Avoid even the suspicion of favouritism for the same reason — that you will lose the very men you seek to keep. Don't be too ready to bring in talent from outside the firm. It may sometimes be necessary; as, for example, when no one on the payroll has the necessary qualifications. But the better policy, where possible, is to look again at the men you have. The man fit for promotion is probably there, but his potential is not always obvious. Look again as if on the assumption that an outside candidate is out of the question, and remember that your other men will be encouraged to think that they will be considered next time. It is true that there will be immediate disappointment and some exchange of snide remarks, but men who know that they have a chance will work better.

If there is ill feeling as a result of an internal promotion you should not simply ignore it. Among the men who feel aggrieved are those who have yet to be promoted and some who have definitely been passed over. Those in the first category should, in turn, be sent away on a course of instruction. This is enough to show them that their claims are being seriously considered. You may find it difficult to do without their services, but the rule is to send the people you cannot spare on courses. One additional and useful result is to test the abilities of the Number Two in each department. Those in the second category may be consoled, in at least some instances, by a lateral move and a change of title. There may be no room for real promotion and some of those concerned may have no special merit other than long service, but even those may deserve some recognition. Goodwill may be bought cheaply through this.

An organization chart is of value in showing people where their responsibilities lie, and also in introducing newcomers to the structure of the firm. But Number One needs another chart, one that is not publicly displayed. This is the chart which shows what would happen if any given executive were to be run over tomorrow. There should be a named successor to everyone shown on the chart: not necessarily his Number Two and not necessarily the man who would fill the longer term vacancy, but the man who would take over immediately and who knows, in outline, what his responsibilities would be. If A were to die (or fall seriously ill), D would take his place. But who will take D's place? His duties would be undertaken by H, in addition to his present duties; and H would also know in outline what he has to do. These emergency plans are essential to any large organization. They serve, moreover, the further purpose of making a man step outside his office and consider the organization as a whole. We often hear these days of conferences and conventions, meetings and seminars, and we query sometimes whether they are worth the time and expense. That is not a question we can decide in the abstract. What is certainly valuable is the experience gained by the deputy when his principal is away. Of that there can be no doubt at all.

In making promotions, there is one further rule and it is this: don't expect the new man to be a replica of the man he is to replace. It is often better in some ways that he should be different. If old A was a strict disciplinarian his successor might well be a little less strict and a shade more popular. If old Z was too easy-going during his last year or two, there is something to be said for a rather tough replacement. There is a useful convention that a man about to retire should have no say in appointing his successor. This is a good rule because the question of what needs to be put right is likely to be considered. Old A and old Z cannot be persuaded that anything is wrong. According to them, their individual departments reached their peak of efficiency on the day of their retirement, all that follows will be an anticlimax. Others may have their own opinions about that but this is not to be discussed while the farewell speeches are being made. The time for a new broom may have come but we'll talk about that after Z has gone.

Making Promises

Talk about hopes and aspirations is all very well. But years and

years later it will be quoted against you. It certainly makes you feel important to throw out promises but don't do it unless you can carry them out to the letter. Even a casual remark about somebody's prospects will be remembered and recorded as something sacred. In fact, meanings will be put into your remarks which you never intended. Misunderstandings like these are not unusual. So it is usually safer to say nothing. In any case never promise anything you can't deliver and make sure no one can possibly think you promised it.

Special News . . .

. . . from a special source and that's what the Big Boss gets. What chance have the others got? No matter how good the son or the nephew or the fifth cousin may be, the others in the works all have an uneasy feeling that the relation is being given special favours. They feel that they never can get a fair deal if someone is giving the Big Boss special news at dinner. So even if young Johnny has the brains of Einstein and the ability of Henry Ford, and no matter how well he does, they'll all say that Papa had a hand in it. Wouldn't it be far better if he were to work somewhere else?

Step One Man Up . . .

. . . and 20 others are bound to be disappointed and they will all ask: 'What about me?' 'What has he got that I haven't?' Such questioning not only happens very often, but it also happens everywhere. The best answer is to take pains to make sure that before you promote someone, the claims of everyone else have been fairly weighed. Are you sure you have considered the case of that quiet little fellow who works in a far away corner of your workshop? Are you sure you have not been led away by the smart young chap who can talk the hind legs off a donkey?

Nothing Ever Goes Right Straightaway

Every effective manager must know that nothing ever goes right straightaway. Invariably something unexpected happens. In fact the one thing which one can confidently expect in a job is that something will go wrong somewhere. The people who work the hardest and the most are the ones who have the expectation that everything will always go right. The reason why they have to work so hard is because they spend so much time unravelling and putting right all the things which have gone wrong and which they did not have the imagination to foresee in the first place.

Effective executives always expect things to go wrong and leave a margin of time to allow for such contingencies. They try their best to ensure that they are never in a hurry, because hurrying only puts people further behind.

The Knowledge Worker Is Becoming More Important Compared to the Manual Worker

There has been a change in emphasis in modern industry from the manual worker to the knowledge worker. For the manual worker, it is relatively easy to have norms and tests to measure the work which he has done. But for the employee whose work comprises his ideas and knowledge, his contribution cannot be closely supervised or checked. He must direct himself. He can only be helped. For a worker of this type — and there are more and more of them in modern industry — thinking is his job and ideas are his products. But his thinking must lead to the production of a better product or a better service or method. Otherwise all the thinking that he has done is entirely useless. Modern industry requires more and more people whose work is 'thinking': the knowledge worker or the man who produces ideas. That is one of the reasons for the great strength of American industry because the USA can afford the enormous cost of producing knowledge workers. A Ph. D. for example represents an investment of over 150,000 dollars. One of the reasons why the USA is rich and powerful is because, in relation to other countries, it has a larger number of knowledge workers as against manual workers.

What Chance Have I Got?

That's what people so often say. If the boss swims or plays bridge with someone's rival in the office, it's difficult to believe that the boss can be entirely fair, even with the best intentions in the world. The wise thing is not to have social relations with the people who report to you in the office. Otherwise, it is bound to lead to heart-burnings.

Leaders who build up first-class executive teams must not, out of necessity, be too close to their immediate subordinates. They can be friendly but they must also keep a distance between themselves and their subordinates. Otherwise their subordinates will tend to work not so much for performance but to conform to what they think the leader requires. Great leaders like Lincoln, Franklin Roosevelt, General Marshall and Sloan all realized the importance of keeping aloof from their subordinates in spite of the fact that many of them were warm men who needed friendship. But they all realized that close friendships and performance do not mix.

This means of course that a chief executive can be appallingly isolated. Everybody wants something from him. There may be no lonelier man than he who sits in the president's chair. His managers want to sell him their ideas or want to advance their own positions. The supplier wants to sell him goods. The customer wants better service at lower prices. The chief executive therefore might find it best to adopt an arm's length attitude towards people in his own defence.

But of course the executive can have good social relations with his equals. They go a long way towards reducing tensions.

Their Serene Imperial Highnesses . . .

Maybe it's an impressive title, but it's astonishing how important titles are in our ordinary day-to-day life. We are all human and we all have our little conceits. What would you like to be called — a 'Clerk' or an 'Administrative Assistant'; a 'Typist' or a 'Secretary'; and 'Office Boy' or a 'General Assistant', a 'Welder' or a 'Welding Specialist'? If you have a complaint, would you like it to be passed to the Complaints Assistant or to the Chairman of the Executive Committee, who is possibly some retired official who does nothing else?

If you are waiting outside an office, who gets in first — the Purchase Officer or the Vice-President of Purchases? Be realistic — think of the joy people get if you give them a nice-sounding title. And it costs nothing!

Scruffy Looking Lot

That's what they are saying and they go on to say that there's no one among them who is really fit for the job higher up and that they must recruit a man from outside. But that's where they could be wrong. Very rarely does a number two or a number three look ready to take on the job of a number one. But give him the responsibility and the odds are that he will do the job extremely well. So give people a chance. They are not indolent and incapable. Maybe they just look that way.

Look at what happened during World War II. Junior clerks, in the course of a few years, ended up being extremely capable Colonels and Brigadiers. Their superiors had been killed and they were given the opportunity. We do well sometimes to recruit from the universities. But there is no need to do this every time. First screen the people in your own organization. Why spend time and money on the selection process when the man you want might be right under your nose?

He is too Busy . . .

. . . you're always told this when you want to send your best people to recruit fresh blood from colleges. But they are precisely the people who must go. What can be a more important task than recruiting the people who will one day run your plant. Surely the best men should be sent.

It's the same with seminars and conferences. Send the people who are too busy to go. They will be the ones who will benefit the most. And there is nothing like getting people out of their own daily routine once in a while for developing their outlook and character.

Who Replaces Whom?

Anyone could be involved any day in a street accident, leaving his work to be done by somebody else. It is important that his temporary successor should be named in advance so that there is

no delay over the replacement. But the one who replaces the injured man will leave a vacancy which someone else must fill. Work out the plan beforehand so as to minimize confusion on the day it happens. We may hope that it won't happen, but we must draw up his chart on the assumption that it will.

Is It All Worthwhile?

That is a difficult question to answer and the answer would not always be the same. However, even if the speeches are pompous and the lectures irrelevant, those attending seminars often learn a lot from each other. They often discover, for example, that the problem they thought peculiar to their own factory has been encountered by everyone else. This is some consolation, even if the

problem remains unsolved. The more certain result of the con-
ference is that the more junior executives are given a taste of
responsibility while their chiefs are away. For the junior who is
apt to criticize those in authority, it is sometimes salutary to find
that he is himself (momentarily) the boss. It can be an unnerving
but useful experience.

The Presentation Clock

On the day of our resignation, we always leave our department in
perfect order: the equipment well maintained, the offices well
staffed and not a single piece of paper in the In-tray. On the day
we take up a new post we always find the plant a shambles, the
machines falling to pieces, the staff quite unsuitable and our desk

littered with unfinished business. It is odd how this should always be so, but we have come to see that it is inevitable.

Appraisals

Many firms have an appraisal system in order to enable them to keep track of the qualities and the work and progress of their employees; but the value of some of these appraisal forms are now being questioned. The theory is that the superior sits down with the person appraised and discusses with the latter his weaknesses and tries to help him rectify them. But in reality, this seldom happens — at any level. The theory seldom works in practice: people just do not sit down quietly and discuss these things. Appraisal forms are usually made out rather hurriedly. They then lie in the files and are seldom looked at.

People are beginning to feel that the concentration of an appraisal form is too often on a man's weaknesses, whereas the important thing should be to concentrate on his strengths.

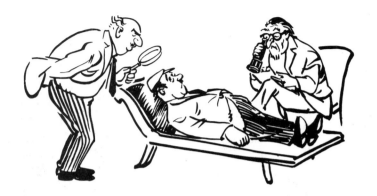

Appraisal forms are seldom interested in bringing out the strengths of an employee and helping him to develop them.

The position in Japan is entirely different. When the Japanese engage a man, they normally engage him permanently until he retires. People are seldom dismissed in Japan. One of the results of this system is that the Japanese do not bother about the weak points of their employees; they are there and have to be accepted. Instead, they try to find out what an employee can do well and then try to help him improve on it. In this manner, they get the maximum benefit out of his strong points.

There is a need, however, for some type of appraisal. Unless one has an appraisal, one is liable, at the last minute, to make a hasty decision when a post has to be filled. As an alternative, perhaps, to the usual appraisal procedure, the following questions could be asked of the persons appraised:

What has he done well?

What does he have to learn or acquire to get the full benefit from his strengths?

If I had a son or a daughter, would I be willing to have him or her work under this person?

(a) If yes, why?

(b) If not, why not?

This might be a far better approach compared to the normal procedure for appraisals.

Concentrate on the Strengths of an Individual

The secret of effective leadership is to work and develop on the strengths of an individual. Individuals have many facets but, for the average individual, there is usually only one area where he might have exceptional abilities. Concentrate on that one area and forget about his weakness because if he is a normal person, he is bound to have them. A man who has no weaknesses is almost certainly bound to be a mediocrity. He is not the leader one is looking for. You simply have to overlook the weaknesses of your men; but make the most use of their strong points. All the well-known leaders and executives of the present and the past had great failings and weaknesses but the important thing — and this is what really matters — is that these people produce results. People without any weaknesses generally produce very little.

9

Paperwork and Red Tape

Administrative and clerical workers multiply by the law of staff proliferation, the rising numbers being unrelated to the work, if any, that has to be done. This fact is generally known, but we have also to realize that rules and regulations multiply in the same way. Any forms devised will become more elaborate as time goes on. Any distribution list will lengthen without any apparent human intervention and every procedure which was originally simple will become complex in the course of time. The complexity is added after the original purpose has been forgotten. Why? It is a sad fact that we are often too lazy to question the usefulness of any accepted procedure. We may grumble about 'red tape' but it is easier to fill in a form than to discover its purpose. We conform to the rules in order to save time and avoid arguments. But it should be the task of the executive to look more critically at paperwork, estimating the cost in clerical time and asking whether that cost is justified. Collecting documents for the record is all very well but business does not exist for the record; it exists to perform a service and to make a profit. While studying any given procedure, we have to ask ourselves whether it actually furthers our aims. If it does not, it should be scrapped. As for collecting all the rules in a policy manual, our best advice to the compiler is 'Don't.' It will probably go out of date in the process of being printed.

Paperwork includes many documents which are not exactly routine. There are reports and memoranda, for example, estimates and cash flow projections. Reports are often essential. They are best given verbally but may be needed in writing. The rule either way is to keep it brief and to the point. It is the lucid explanation that makes the big impact, while long-winded documents are rejected on principle. As for memoranda, their indiscriminate use can degenerate into a paper war, which is the last thing we want to encourage. Budgets and estimates are an essential tool of management but are often misused, being made the occasion for argument about trifling items of expenditure and being often compiled as a sort of ritual and thereafter ignored and filed for reference. Last to be considered are travel expense accounts, which can involve clerks in a great deal of detailed work. The tendency here is to spend more on preventing dishonesty than the dishonesty itself could possibly cost. The better policy is to trust people because of two reasons. In the first place, they are mostly honest. In the second place, it would still be cheaper even if they weren't.

At the Drop of a Hat

. . . he will go ahead and create another form. You'll be astonished at the number of forms which the average organization has. Many of them are entirely unnecessary and an enormous amount of time is wasted filling them up. The creation and use of forms should be carefully controlled.

People start a procedure with very little hesitation and it goes on and on, month after month, year after year, long after the need for this procedure has passed. The surprising thing is that it is far easier to start a procedure than to stop it.

There is the interesting example of a big company which suspended all reports and forms for two months. After that, only those forms which the manager actually asked for were allowed to return. In this way, the reports and forms of this particular company were actually reduced by as much as three quarters!

Reports and procedures should focus only on what is needed to achieve results in the coming years. A multiplicity of reports only confuse — and sometimes they actually misdirect.

First One Post . . .

. . . is created. Then the secretary, the office boy, the assistant, the clerk, the typist, and so it goes on. Our experience is always proving the truth of Parkinson's Law; that work expands to fill the time available; that office staff will multiply, irrespective of the work (if any) to be done. Nor are the redundant people idle because they make work for each other. Staff proliferation is not only difficult to prevent but it has many evil results. First of all, it is a waste of money. Second, it is a waste of time. Third, it results in the work being badly done. Watch out for staff proliferation and be ready to say 'No!'

112

Are Procedures More Important?

. . . or is it not more important to turn out more products of better quality and at cheaper cost? The answer is obvious, you will say. But you'll be surprised at the emphasis that is so often put on following a procedure to the letter. The result is you are completely tied up with red tape. You must, of course, have rules and regulations if your organization is to run properly, but don't be a slave to them. If you find matters getting out of hand, it is time to change the rules.

The Order of Names . . .

. . . on memos, circulars, notices. You cannot imagine how upset people can be when they see that their own names are lower than some of the others. It is always a tricky business and it always causes heart-burnings. Very often it's not certain, and it cannot be certain, as to who is higher or lower than whom in a hierarchy.

So if you want to avoid this source of friction, it is best to make sure that whenever any memoranda go out, the circulation list should be in alphabetical order.

Factors Responsible for the Great Success of Marks and Spencers

- Perhaps one of the main reasons for the success of Marks and Spencers is that the owners were very clear as to what their objectives were: and this enabled them to work single-mindedly towards fulfilling them. The objective they settled on was to make a social revolution: to provide upper class clothes of good quality at prices which middle and working classes could afford.

- Another objective of Marks and Spencers is always to have high productivity. Both these objectives have been attained. The sales per square foot of floor area in Marks and Spencers are far greater than in any other department store in the world and the reason for this is their high productivity standards.

- Marks and Spencers make a realistic appraisal of everything.

They refused to accept anything just because it existed. If something was no longer profitable or of little use, they abandoned it straightaway no matter how much time, money, prestige and effort they might have invested in it.

- In the UK, they have been the most successful in the reduction of procedures and paperwork. They have reduced paperwork to the minimum by subjecting their procedures to continual scrutiny and this has resulted in greater savings in expenditure.

- Detailed records of each item of stores, where movement in and out of each item of material was noted, had been done away with altogether in all the numerous branches of the organization. At the time, when this was done, it was considered a dangerous decision but actual experience proved it to be entirely correct. It was found that the amount of goods stolen through not having detailed stock records had been more than offset by the enormous saving in costs through not having so much detailed and expensive paperwork.

   Over 30 million pieces of paper forms, cards etc. and the queries that were inseparable from paperwork were entirely eliminated.

115

- Staff do not clock in and out. This is not only a big boost for their morale but it has also led to great savings in cards and statistics and, interestingly enough, not to a deterioration in punctuality compared to the previous position when everyone clocked in and out.

- If a branch manager wishes to purchase something, he goes ahead and gets it straightaway by buying it locally, whilst formerly he had to indent it from a main central store. This has not only avoided a great deal of frustration and an enormous amount of paperwork but it has also led to speedy action.

- By looking at everything more realistically, internal audit staff has been cut to almost half.

- This realistic approach to everything means that in spite of an enormous increase in business, the number of employees handling the work has not gone up.

- In every organization, rapid staff turnover inevitably leads to considerable additional expenditure though of course, it is difficult to evaluate the extent of this expenditure. New staff cannot possibly be as productive as staff that has had some months or years of experience. New staff needs to be trained and training costs money. Recruitment and interviewing of staff is also a time-consuming and expensive business. It has been roughly estimated in the USA that the average executive represents an investment by an organization of about $50,000 after, say, eight years of service. Where an organization employs a large number of girls, staff turnover is always much greater. Staff turnover is low at Marks and Spencers because of the excellent facilities they offer: beautifully fitted rest rooms with piped music, hair dressing facilities, manicures, subsidized lunches and so on. And the cost of all this was more than offset by the savings brought about due to low staff turnover.

- Another area where Marks and Spencers have made a big departure from existing practices is in their treatment of their

MARKS AND SPENCERS

suppliers of goods and services. Traditionally, suppliers have always been regarded suspiciously and sometimes even with a slight element of hostility. But, at Marks and Spencers, suppliers are cultivated and treated as friends. They are helped at every stage with regard to specifications, quality and sometimes, even with finance. But, above all else, the prospects of very large and continuing orders have always been a very great help and encouragement to them.

What Are Profits?

Profits are not just something nice to have or a goal to be aimed at. Profits are a necessity. Without profits, an organization will wither and die. You will be surprised to know that among the large number of companies that show profits in their published accounts, many are really not making any profits at all. Let us explain.

Factor of obsolescence

In these times of rapid technological advances, obsolescence of plant and machinery is an important factor and unless one keeps abreast with the latest equipment, not only will the cost of the products made be higher than that of one's competitors, but the quality will also not be as good. It is not yet properly realized that

PROFIT & LOSS

an obsolete plant, in the long run, is an expensive plant. So it is essential that the profit figures make sufficient provision for periodical replacement of obsolete machinery with newer models.

Influence of inflation

Then there is the important factor of inflation. Profits must provide for the replacement of assets. An asset which has been purchased a few years earlier not only becomes obsolete but, because of inflation, its replacement costs go up enormously. The probability is that the amount set aside by way of depreciation which is normally based on the original cost of purchase is grossly unrealistic and quite insufficient.

Taxes have to be provided for

A business, after all, exists in a society and that entails social costs such as schools, roads, hospitals, water supply systems and so on. An organization must, therefore, make sufficient profits to pay the taxes which these social costs entail and still have enough to stay in business.

118

Sufficient profits to attract capital

Unless an organization expands, it will stagnate and die. So profits must be the means by which an enterprise gets additional capital for the expansion of its business. If an investor is going to invest his money in a business, the first thing he will do is to examine the profitability of that enterprise over the years, both past and future and see how this profitability compares with that of the other enterprises. Unless the profit prospects are good, he will shy away and invest elsewhere where the profitability is higher. The enterprise will thereby be starved of the additional capital which is so necessary for its survival.

Factor of risk

In business there is always a factor of risk. Take, for example, an oil company which may spend millions of dollars over a period of years on exploration. Much of this expenditure may well be infructuous, but one gusher will more than make up for all the money spent. Hence, there must be an element in profits to cover the numerous risk factors that face every organization.

It is not good enough just to consider the profits of a calendar year. The profit picture must be looked at over a period of years. Some are bad years and some are good. So the profits earned must cover the lean years. A yearly profit, as such, is misleading unless we know for how many years a profit can be expected. We should, therefore, always try to work out the anticipated profits over the life of an investment.

Profits are a necessity

It is clear from what we have said that profit is the premium which must be paid to meet all these factors. It could almost be regarded as an item of 'expenditure'. Profit is quite definitely a necessity. Unless an organization earns a sufficient amount of profits, it will not be able to survive in the long run.

So it can be seen that even if angels instead of businessmen sat in the chairs of the directors' boardroom, there would still be a need for profits despite the lack of their personal interest in making profits.

Profitability is based on capital employed

Profit is still the best gauge for assessing the success or failure of a business and also for comparisons with other businesses. But this is an area which can mislead. For example, the percentage of profit on sales is often used as a guide regarding profitability but this can give an incomplete picture as it takes no account of the amounts invested, or the overheads involved.

In the circumstances, perhaps the best gauge of profitability would be profit on capital employed. But here again, there are complications which might make comparisons misleading. The dollar invested in 1950 is very different from that invested in 1985.

There is, then, no entirely satisfactory method for comparing profitability between one organization and another. But, in spite of all its disadvantages, profit on capital employed probably gives the best indication of profitability. When such comparisons are made, care should be taken to ensure that the actual calculation of capital employed is done on a uniform basis and that factors such as depreciation are worked out on a like with like basis.

Management and profits are quite separate matters

Managing a business and the quantum of profits made by a business are two entirely separate matters. But in the popular mind, profits and the running and functioning of a business are very closely connected. This concept, which is prevalent to the public mind, is not only entirely erroneous but has also done much harm to industrial society. This is due to the fact that the public has not been able to distinguish between a fair profit and profiteering. This indiscriminate hostility to profit has been largely responsible for some of the worst mistakes in public policy throughout the world.

'Not According to the Rules'

'It's against our policy.' 'It doesn't concern this section.' A policy

manual is often used to stifle and kill imaginative ideas, sometimes to such an extent that it will put off and depress anyone with any spark of initiative in him. If policy manuals are written in general terms, they serve no purpose. If they are specific, they are usually out of date. Think twice, therefore, before you start a manual.

His Missus Will Never Understand It

That's what Bill is thinking. He cannot understand it himself. He has been told it has been worked out very efficiently on the new computer, giving details of all his deductions and also his incentive bonus. But he finds the mass of details impossible to understand. It is all too complicated. It might be a very efficient and economic way of working out the pay slip but it has entirely ignored the human and emotional factors. What's the use of a very efficient incentive scheme if it doesn't make sense to Bill?

You can have the most efficient system in the world but if it's incomprehensible to those who are very much concerned with it, then it's certainly not the best way of getting something done.

How to Win Your Point

Bulky reports and long notes are no good if you want to convince anyone. Don't prepare long reports. Few people will read them and fewer still will understand them. Those who want to oppose the project will have read enough to squash it.

So if you want to convince anyone, be brief and to the point.

Did You Know . . .

. . . that during the Second World War, when the War and Supply Ministry of a certain country was in conflict it was said that over 25% of its staff were employed just in writing memoranda directed at each other? Memoranda are usually written by people who want to have alibis, if something goes wrong. They then produce them at the drop of a hat to protect themselves.

Memoranda are all right if you want to distribute information which no one is going to argue over. But insist that there's nothing in them which can lead to a paper war because that does nobody any good. It's far better not to have memoranda of this type at all — you'll then have an atmosphere of mutual trust which is so much more important.

You'll Be Surprised . . .

. . . but in many companies a budget is treated in the same way. It is put into cold storage. It's often treated as a chore: the previous year's figures are picked up and a few additions or subtractions are made. The budget is inflated to the extent that the executives can get away with it. (Later there's much joy because the budget shows underspending.) The budget is then sent off to top management. A copy is filed; and everyone heaves a sigh of relief. They then get on with their normal day-to-day work. This approach is unfortunate because a budget can be a most effective management tool:

- Budgets are actually future action plans of an organization. These plans are expressed in terms of money and are made for the current year and often also for many years ahead. Budgeting for the future makes people think and forces them to plan ahead and to anticipate problems.

- A budget also helps to tell you how you are progressing against your plans because it shows you how the expenditure actually incurred compares with the expenditure which was planned. These comparisons are often made month by month.

- In fact, the key to control is through budgets. For every item of expenditure to be incurred, there just must be a budget or a plan; and the expenditure actually incurred must be compared periodically with the plan. Unless you have a budget, expenditure is very likely to get out of hand.

- The important thing is not to be overwhelmed by the figures in a budget. Concentrate on the big value items. You will find that they are usually few in number but they make up the bulk, perhaps seventy-five per cent, of the total expenditure. This is a useful approach because you will be amazed at the number of people who waste time and effort over items of relatively small value: effort which they could have well spent much more usefully by paying attention to the big value items. For the small value items, which are large in numbers, it would be quite satisfactory to work on some general overall average figures so that little time is spent on them.

- A budget must not be prepared by some smart young men at the head office, in collaboration with the people who are directly concerned with the working of the budget.

124

- Another thing to remember about budgets and all such financial statements is that it must be written in a language which is understandable: even words such as 'higher' or 'lower' can cause confusion because one is not always certain what is being referred to. Why not use 'better' or 'worse'?

- Perhaps the biggest confusion of all is caused when one compares figures between one period and another and when these figures are not on a similar basis. Changes in the conventions of accounting or in the period of time concerned can make such comparisons very misleading.

When He Gets Back . . .

. . . the first thing he will do will be to make up his Travel Expense Account. Here is an area which often gives rise to great controversy. Some companies have an elaborate system of check and double-check. This not only takes up a lot of time but it often costs more than the fiddling and acts as a challenge to people to see how much they can get away with.

The other approach would be to trust people more. In the long run, this might be much cheaper. It will not only reduce the cost of checking but it might also lessen tension all round, which in itself would be worth big money. And if people are trusted more, they usually make an effort to deserve that trust.

Flexible . . .

. . . but they are more than that. They have that little something which makes a person's heart jump a beat or two when they see them. We have to be flexible in our attitudes too. Things are continually changing — new systems, new ideas, new circumstances. Don't be hide-bound. Have a flexible approach and adapt yourself to changing conditions.

Important Elements of Cost Which Are Sometimes Not Taken Fully into Account

Some of the costs of a business such as packaging, storage, transportation, distribution and movement — all of which, taken together, can be very high — are often shown under the heading 'miscellaneous' in the accounts of a company, or merged under

many different accounts. The result is that they cannot be properly controlled as the accounting system would not normally bring out these costs separately as one activity and in one account. Therefore these costs tend to become 'hidden' in various different accounts.

The significant thing, however, is that the type of expenditure which we have noted above lends itself much more readily to cost reduction efforts than the expenditure which is incurred in the actual manufacture of products. The reason for this is that manufacturing costs have always had the bulk of the trained force of industrial engineers centered on them, with the result that there is relatively little scope for further cost reduction. But expenditure such as packaging, storage, movement, transportation, cost of finance are usually scattered in many different accounts and they tend to become hidden and forgotten. Therefore, this type of expenditure lends itself very readily to cost reduction efforts and,

127

can be very considerable if examined by an operations research team or by systems engineers.

Uncoupling certain operations

In many process industries, as in the case of aluminium rolling or paper making there may be considerable waste in some areas if all the processes are integrated and have to work together. Some of these items of equipment will be working but not processing anything. Big cost reductions may be achieved by uncoupling some of the manufacturing and finishing processes.

Cost of distribution

The cost of distribution may amount to very big money especially where there is a very large number of retailers. These costs also sometimes tend to become hidden under different accounts. Sometimes there may even be a good financial case for dropping a large number of the small retailers altogether and concentrating on the bigger ones who bring in the bulk of the money.

Cost of finance

An interest charge is made for the use of money borrowed: in addition, for the use of common stock money which is acquired for starting and running a business, profits in the form of dividends have to be paid to the shareholders. Interest charges and dividends are among the biggest elements of 'cost' of a business. And yet it is only recently that management has really given some serious attention to this important element of 'expenditure' although few things are as expensive as the wrong financial structure. For example, if an organization issues common stock to meet a temporary requirement of money, this is an expensive way of getting finance. It would be far more economical to take a bank loan. Interest charges on a bank loan cost much less than paying dividends because interest, unlike dividends, is allowed as a deduction for tax purposes. Moreover a loan can always be returned if it is no longer required and then taken up again when it is required. It is not permanent like increasing common stock.

Cost of not doing or idle time

The cost of not doing, or idle time, can be very high. For example, in the case of a machine which is idle for some time, the expenditure for that machine remains the same even though fewer products are manufactured. And, of course, the profits lost from the goods not made are virtually a cost as well. This applies equally to many other areas of activity. In technical jargon this is called 'lost opportunity costs'. For example, a jet plane can have many empty seats because there has not been a proper rescheduling of routes. A freighter can spend many days in a port loading and unloading because material handling arrangements are not satisfactory. A cargo ship can return empty because its programme has not been planned well in advance. These are all areas of big 'lost opportunity costs' which the accounts records can never show up separately.

Cost of movement

Management experts have estimated that the cost of movement of an engineering product can often be as high as 30% of the total cost of the product. You will be astonished at the amount of movement which you do in fact have in an average engineering works. Hundreds of different types of materials come in. Scores of separate parts are being manufactured. Each part may have up to five or six separate operations performed on it. Sometimes each operation has to be inspected. Then there is warehousing. All this involves movement and movement means expenditure. To reduce this expenditure it is important to pay a great deal of attention to the layout of the factory right from the start and also to ensure that the movement of material follows the straightest possible path.

Policing Costs

'Policing' might be a strange word to use in connection with costs, but a great deal of expenditure can be incurred on 'policing' in an average organization. Take, for example, inspection and checking in some organizations, every item is inspected and checked and this is done at great cost. After all, one single engineering product, say a truck, may contain over 3,000 separate parts and many parts may have to have five to six separate operations of work done on it. So, as you can imagine, the cost of checking and inspecting every single operation of work can be staggering. But this is where management skill comes in: a representative sampling should be done at random and this should be checked thoroughly. If this check indicates that everything is all right, then it would be reasonable to assume that the remainder is also correct. These are not easy decisions. But they are decisions where management experience and acumen can save enormous sums of money.

The same principle also applies to auditing. Here again, a sensible management approach may save big sums of money and an expensive auditing staff can be considerably reduced without any real diminution in effectiveness.

Buying Is As Important As Selling . . .

. . . if not more important than selling, and the best selling cannot make up for mediocre buying. But buying doesn't just mean purchasing; it means integrating the design, the availability of material, the type of material and also the simplest and least expensive way of doing a particular job. That is why many go-ahead organizations have a very senior materials manager who helps to co-ordinate and integrate all the buying and related functions.

The example on page 131 is representative of many organizations. Normal accounting records would never bring out this type of analysis. It will be noted that depreciation and maintenance are shown as 'cost of money': this is due to the fact that depreciation is virtually a return of money which has been invested in one lump sum for purchase of equipment; and maintenance represents the cost of keeping this equipment in good working order. Profits have also been shown under the heading 'cost of money' as profits are actually the cost of capital needed to stay in the business.

130

ABC COMPANY INCORPORATED
COST STRUCTURE

The sales dollar   100%

1. Physical movement of materials and goods:

   a. From supplier to factory; from stores to
      machines; and movement through the factory
      from one production centre to another   7%

   b. From machines as finished goods through
      crating, packaging, shipping, warehousing
      and to the distributors   5%

   c. By distributors (wholesale and retail)   6%

   Total cost of movement   18%

2. Cost of money

   a. Working capital, interest charges,
      depreciation and maintenance of equipment   12%

   b. Money locked up with wholesalers and retailers   7%

   c. Profits before taxes of manufacturer,
      wholesaler and retailer (but not counting
      the profits of suppliers of materials as
      this figure is most difficult to ascertain)   10%

   Total cost   29%

3. Purchase of materials and supplies   24%

4. Manufacturing - cost of converting materials
   into finished goods   10%

5. Administration and accounting (manufacturer,
   wholesaler and retailer)   9%

6. Selling and sales promotion (manufacturer,
   wholesaler and retailer)   7%

7. Investment in research and development, market
   development, executive development, etc.   3%

Sales dollar as above   100%

Managers do not fully realize the important part played by 'movement' and 'finance' in their costs. Such an analysis will help them to make a reduction in these costs and this can certainly be done by careful thinking.

Costs Common to Many Products Must Be Properly Distributed

This matter is especially important because a big proportion of today's expenditure — other than direct materials — cannot be directly attached to a particular product but is common to all the products being manufactured by an organization. Faulty distribution of this common expenditure can give a completely misleading profit and loss picture of a product. The distribution of the common expenditure must be done according to the circumstances. In some cases, it might be best to distribute certain types of expenditure on the basis of the number of invoices sent out; in others it might be on shipments despatched; for department stores, it might be on the basis of the purchases per customer. In companies making computers it might be on the number of proposals made. So in an extrusion plant, the appropriate unit of transaction might be the number of skilled die-maker — hours needed to prepare the presses for any one specific mould. For commercial airlines the most meaningful cost unit would be the number of seat-miles available. These are just some examples showing how common costs should be distributed. Only if they are done in such a manner can you get a realistic picture of your operations.

There have been cases where products have been shown in the books as being profitable whilst, in fact, they have been entirely unprofitable simply because the distribution of the numerous items of common expenditure such as warehousing, maintenance, handling materials and purchasing charges — over the various types of products manufactured by the organization — has not been done correctly. This happens oftener than one thinks because organizations tend to be fairly rigid about the systems which they adopt for the distribution of items of common expenditure.

Items of 'common' expenditure all add up to very big figures. As this expenditure is 'common' to many of the products being made in an organization, special care should be taken to ensure that it is properly allocated or distributed over the various products manufactured. This 'common' expenditure should be distributed over the different products made in an organization on the basis of estimated *use* of this expenditure óver the various products manufactured. Any other method of distribution of these common' costs would give a misleading profit/loss picture of the different items manufactured.

For example, one product may be high in value but small in weight and requiring very little effort by way of packaging, storing and despatch. Conversely, another product may be inexpensive but heavy, requiring a considerable amount of handling and packaging. In this case clearly the expenditure on packaging and movement should be spread on the basis of the weight or bulk of the product and not on the basis of cost. Or in other words on the basis of use. You will be surprised at the number of organizations that distribute their expenditure on the basis of cost. But very often, as shown by the example just given, this gives an entirely misleading profit and loss picture. Distribution of common expenditure must be in accordance with the use made of those items of common expenditure.

10

Consulting People

There can be only one chief executive and it is he who must make the big decisions. That does not mean, however, that he reaches each decision unaided. There are two reasons why the wise executive will never decide without first taking the opinions of his more senior executives: one being that they like to be consulted and the other being that their advice may be valuable. They may all offer the same advice and he may well decide to reject it, but at least he knows why they differ from him and why he must overrule them. That is a very different thing from ignoring everybody. The Napoleonic attitude can backfire, especially if you happen to be less than Napoleonic in genius.

Once decisions have been taken, they have to be explained to others. People are unlikely to be influenced by the making of speeches. Few are convinced by argument and fewer still by angry words and bullying. Some can be persuaded, but the real secret is to build up a reputation for sincerity. People turn, in the end, to a man they have learnt to trust. Remember, however, that trust is based only on past experience. If you have arranged to meet your friend somewhere and there is no sign of him as the appointed hour approaches, your wife may say: 'Perhaps he has forgotten,' to which you will perhaps reply: 'I have known Joe for twenty years, and he has never yet failed to keep an appointment — and, look, there he is!' The point you are making is not that you like Joe, nor that he is your friend, but that he always keeps his word. You are not depending on what he has said but upon what he has always done. This reputation has to be built up over the years. It is no good saying 'I am to be trusted.' You have to prove it beforehand, earning the trust of the people you employ. You are then in a position to persuade them. They will believe, from the outset, that what you say is true. It may take ten years to establish the sort of reputation that will induce people to trust you.

When consulting your senior executives, asking them separately for their opinions is a very wise precaution: to ask their opinions at a mass meeting is far less productive. You will, in that way, obtain the views of the crackpot, the buffoon and the rebel, but the more sensible people are those least likely to talk in public. The situation is rather like that embarrassing scene when television interviewers try to sample public opinion on the current crisis, obtaining nothing but stuttered and semi-audible signs of confusion. To know what the employees are thinking, you would do better to have a talk with old Tom, the fitter, or old Kate of the works canteen; people whose views are probably representative and who have had the chance to hear what the others are saying.

If you seek the advice of other people who are not in the business — a banker or a lawyer — remember that however talented these learned professionals are, they have no real grasp of a central fact in business: that your project can end in a loss of money. People like civil servants may have known disappointment, as in being bypassed for promotion and being asked to retire before their time, but they know little about business risks. They cannot readily envisage a situation where the expected profit is unexpectedly small. They seldom remember that the money invested can actually be lost beyond recovery. The businessman is almost alone in considering loss as a normal incident in life. Therefore, advice from anyone not in business can be wrong in that they are too optimistic.

One other possibility you may consider is to engage the services of a business consultant or industrial engineer. You may feel that this is an admission of weakness and you may well ask how a self-appointed expert can know more about your business than you do. The point is, he can't, but you would probably have to resort to a consultant at a moment of crisis, when the decision to be made is of the first importance. For instance, you are threatened with a take-over bid; or you have the chance to buy out a rival firm; or the moment has come, perhaps, to diversify the firm's products. The decision to be made may be of a sort which will confront you only once in a lifetime. The consultant may not have great experience in your particular business but he may have great experience of your particular type of crisis. Remember that almost all his work is with firms which are confronted with a momentous decision which may require a complete re-organization. He is not called in to advise on matters of routine. It is only the difficult situations that he ever sees, with the result that he gains a wide knowledge of a particular range of problems such as those which may arise in a particular industry. Such a consultant might help you a great deal. You need, however, to choose your adviser with care. The profession of business consultancy is a relatively new one with qualifications and rules still to be established. It includes some people of undoubted ability, but it also includes other folks whose advice is of less obvious value. Choice of the right consultant may sometimes be as difficult a problem as the one the consultant will be called in to solve.

It is right to seek advice within the firm, and it may sometimes be right to employ a professional adviser, but the decision must ultimately be made by the chief executive, whose whole career may be in the balance. On him rests the burden of responsibility and there is no escape from it. Having studied the facts and listed the options, having weighed the chances and considered the dangers, he makes his decision, sometimes against the advice and opinion of some or all of his senior executives. His choice over-rules theirs and will be the policy which the company will follow. However, its success or failure will not be a matter of opinion. It will be shown beyond argument in the unforgiving figures of the balance sheet. Such a crucial decision is difficult to make but the making of it is one of the services — and perhaps the most important service — for which the chief executive is paid.

The Peerless Leader . . .

. . . the little Napoleon. That's how he fancies himself. He never uses the opinions and ideas of his men. But one day he will have a real fall and get pushed off to St. Helena. Remember, your men have ideas and brains as well. Surely, four minds on one job are better than one and it gives everyone a feeling of being part of a team, all working together.

Just Don't Imagine . . .

. . . that they are taking in everything you say. The average person is much smarter than you imagine. And he thinks just as much as you do about the problems that concern him. Don't imagine that you can throw dust in his eyes. He'll spot it soon enough. The best way to handle people is to be sincere and honest.

Foolish to Try

No one has ever convinced anyone by an argument. Your case can be 100% cast-iron. In spite of that you'll never win over anyone through arguing if he doesn't want to be convinced. There's a bit of a lawyer in everyone's breast; they'll always come out with some sort of argument — no matter how absurd. So take it easy. Be calm and open-minded. You've got to win people's hearts not their minds. Then you might have some chance of getting them to agree with you. But you will never win them over by cold logic and reason.

138

'Would You Mind?'

People would much prefer an order given to them to be prefaced like this. If you probe deep down, you'll find that most people hate having anyone in authority over them. But you must always have a leader if you want to get things done efficiently. The most effective boss, however, is the one who carries his authority lightly and doesn't throw his weight around. It is no use asking people to trust you, for it is not in their power to do so. They either trust you or they don't. If they trust you it is because they have known you for years and have discovered that you are to be trusted. What you have told them has always been the truth. What you have promised, you have always fulfilled. Any appointments you have made, you have always kept. In this instance Joe has agreed to meet the Boss at the airport, bringing with him the report which the Boss means to read during the journey and which is to be used at the meeting he is to attend soon after landing. The Boss knows that Joe will be there as arranged because Joe, in his experience, has never been late for an appointment. Trust is something which you have to earn. If people do not

trust you it may be because they do not know you. They may distrust you because you have let them down in the past. Or else,
they may distrust you because you talk too much and do too
little. It is worthwhile asking yourself whether you inspire trust —
and if not, why not?

No One Ever Wins . . .

. . . if only more people realized this. It's only very seldom that
you can crush anyone completely. Yet so many people want to
rush into battle. There are occasions, of course, when there is no
choice except to demonstrate definitely who is the boss — but

these are rare. In most cases a battle and its awful aftermath could have been avoided with a little self-control and a little patience.

What Do You Think Of . . .

A weakness in democratic theory is that we are too often asking the opinion of people who know too little to have formed one. Many problems of the present day — scientific, technical, economic and financial — are quite beyond the man in the street. It is not a case of his being mistaken, or being deceived by his newspaper. It is neither a case of his repeating a proverbial saying learnt from his grandmother. So, far from giving a silly answer, he has not even understood the question. He has no opinion nor

141

the means of forming one. We would do well, therefore, to avoid the pretence of sampling the views of people who have no views at all. The exercise is futile, at best, and is often dishonest.

Let's Ask Old Tom

There is an old Tom in every factory, a man who has been in the firm for years and who is known and liked by everyone. What Tom says is a reflection of what the rest are thinking. He is a typical workman but his long service allows him to be a little more outspoken than the rest. The supervisor has found that it pays to have coffee with Tom about once a month. In this instance, he wants to know how people are reacting to the new computerized pay slips. Tom's opinion is sure to be typical. But the factory employs women as well as men. So the supervisor consults old Kate at the same time, partly because she gives the woman's point of view, and partly because she knows what people are saying in the canteen. Neither Tom nor Kate will tell tales but they help the supervisor to keep in touch.

Consultants Are More Useful in the Upper Hierarchy

The story goes that a business consultant was called in to study the everyday routine of a firm's general office. In one corner he found a clerk looking idly out of the window. 'What are you doing?' he asked, to which the clerk truthfully replied: 'Nothing.' The consultant made a note and presently found another clerk in the opposite corner, obviously just as idle. Questioned as in the previous case, the clerk admitted that he was doing nothing. 'A clear instance of overlapping!' cried the consultant in triumph. It is rather doubtful whether this sort of consultation achieves much in the reduction of overheads. The consultant's final advice is usually to set up an Organization and Method Department, which is itself subject to the law of staff proliferation. The consultant is perhaps more useful on the higher level, in advising on the top management structure or whether to manufacture a new product or whether to merge with another firm.

Passing the Buck

Passing the buck is a bad practice, more so when the matter is merely passed on without any recommendation or advice. There are matters, nevertheless, on which the chief executive's decision is essential. It is also final. In the last resort the responsibility is his.

But this is where his management skill comes in, or else everyone will pass on their problems to him for a decision. Once a problem is passed on, the managers can settle back and relax. The ball is now in the chief executive's court. But this must be resisted. Continual management effort is required to see that decisions are to be carried out. Responsibility and authority must be decentralized as much as possible. Otherwise everything will slowly come to a standstill. The head office will have far too much to do — and the men in the branch offices will become frustrated because of the lack of any real responsibility.

11

A Decision Is Usually a Judgement

A decision is usually a choice between various feasible alternatives. The higher one rises, the pros and cons between the alternative courses of action for which a choice has to be made are usually almost equally balanced. If it were otherwise, somebody else lower down would, or should have made the decision. One should take as many opinions as one can, and then, based on these various opinions, a decision should be arrived at. We have specially mentioned that decisions should be based on opinions, and not facts, because in many cases, a fact itself is not clear and can be very misleading if it is not viewed in the right context. And there is often a great temptation to find facts that can prove one's own point of view.

The effective leader encourages different opinions. In fact, if he finds that most of his subordinates agree on a certain line of action, he might not even take a decision at all, because he prefers to base his judgement on a number of varying opinions

Most of the good decision makers of history like to arrive at a decision after they have first listened to all the different points of view. An interesting example of decision-making is that of Franklin Roosevelt who used unorthodox methods to arrive at a decision. He used to take the opinions of very many persons and often played off one person's opinion against another. His methods went slap against all the normal canons of administration. But Roosevelt, being the clever man he was, realized that the most important job of a President was not administration or methods, but policies. It was the right policy that really mattered — and not how that right policy was arrived at.

It Is Not At All Absurd

You'll be surprised how often this sort of thing takes place in real life. Even if there is a crisis, you will find managers failing to take action simply because they have not obtained clearance from above. Decision-making should be delegated right down to the scene of an action as far as possible. Only then can the management be effective. This is well illustrated by one of the most heroic blunders ever made: the famous Charge of the Light Brigade in the Crimean War was ordered by someone many kilometres away from the scene of action — no officer in his senses who was actually at the site would ever have given such a stupid order. But in those days, they did not believe in delegating powers right down to the scene of action.

The normal manager works under continuous pressure. He's often in a position where he has to take a decision without having access to all the facts. Sometimes he has to decide without being covered by the necessary authority. But it's the fellow that takes the plunge and makes a decision irrespective of whether or not he has adequate clearance who's the real manager. He's the chap who has it in him. He will go way ahead of the timid ones in the long run.

What Does Operations Research Mean?

Operations research is a high sounding term which is often used when people want to make an impression. Actually the term is a bit of a misnomer because it is neither 'operations' nor 'research'. There is really nothing very new about operations research. It is the application of common sense principles and these principles must have been used as long ago as when they built the Great Wall of China. The new thing about operations research, compared to what happened in the past, is the use of the computer and also certain mathematical and logical techniques.

How Does It Help Decision-Making?

- It first finds out the resources which will be needed for the various alternative methods in which a problem can be solved.

- It then works out the most economical way in which a solution can be arrived at. For example, to take an extreme case, there is no point in using a rocket gun to shoot down sparrows.

- The risks, the limitations and the probabilities of each of the alternative methods of handling a problem are then weighed.

- Operations research can bring together the contribution and the functions of all the various aspects of an organization and show their total impact on the results of the entire business.

As we have already said, all the above things have been done in the past for generations by people with intelligence. But at the present, operations research has systematized such techniques, thereby helping people to make decisions with a high degree of rationality by taking into account the risks, the future and the resources that are available.

Most of us in our work use operations research techniques in one way or another perhaps without realizing it. This technique can be used for the planning of a big sophisticated factory or for the making of a simple cup of tea.

For example, if a housewife invites seventeen people to her home, chances are some of her guests will drink tea and some coffee. There is a certain amount of tea and coffee in the house and the housewife would like to economize on the total expenditure as much as possible. Between tea and coffee, coffee is the more expensive. She knows that among her guests there are five who will drink only coffee. And therefore this wise housewife decides to make the minimum number of five cups of coffee. But she does not have enough tea for the remaining 12 guests and so a 'constraint' arises. There is enough tea only for 10 guests. So she will finally make 7 cups of coffee and 10 cups of tea. This is a good example of 'operations research' which entails making the best and the most economical use of the resources available, or to use technical jargon 'optimization in the face of constraints'.

Crisis Management

Making a decision, hesitating over it, changing it the next day and deciding on something else the next — this is what is known as crisis management. It results from a failure to learn from past mistakes. Under good management, a routine is established which enables people of limited intelligence to do work which was once left to the highly skilled.

A well managed factory is a quiet place. Nothing exciting ever happens there because everything has been anticipated and made into a routine.

Where crisis management prevails, the work of every one comes to a stop of weeks on end and then they spend a great deal of time trying to catch up on their arrears, with everything being done badly. Therefore a successful manager must endeavour to organize his work in such a way that he anticipates a crisis and thus avoids it. He tries to make everything into a routine. The important concern of an organization is planning for the future and not time-taking mopping-up operations because of the crisis decisions which were made in the past.

The Pentagon used to work from one crisis to another: things usually reaching a crescendo of activity at the end of every financial year. The famous McNamara eliminated the need for much of this crisis activity simply by no longer insisting that expenditure appropriated for the year be spent in that year alone. McNamara allowed unspent expenditure to be used in the succeeding year. It was as simple as that. But it avoided a great deal of crisis activity and therefore saved everybody's time.

Some Thoughts on Decision-Making

An executive should not have to make too many decisions. If he does, it is a certain indication that his organization is faulty and that he is working under day to day pressures and is continuously patching up. It is not the right approach to take each case on its merits and to deal with it. The important thing is to try to find out the underlying causes behind the separate occurrences. It will be found, on an analysis of these occurrences, that there are certain constant factors. From these constant factors, principles can be evolved and a decision can be arrived which will cover all these common occurrences. This then becomes what is termed as a generic or strategic decision; such decisions are not problem-solving; they tackle matters at the highest conceptual level of understanding and they are not adaptations to the apparent needs of the moment. They try to ascertain the constant factors that underlie a great many occurrences so that it can be settled by a principle or, in other words, by a generic decision.

For example, you may have many leakages in the steam piping of a factory. These steam leaks in various places are constantly being patched up. But when the total workload is analysed over some months, then the generic problem appears. They find that the temperatures and pressures have become too great for the existing equipment and that all the couplings holding together the different lines need to be redesigned for the greater loads. Until this is done, a great deal of time and expense will be spent fixing the leaks and there will be no proper control of the situation.

Effective executives have to know when a decision is to be a generic or strategic one and when a pragmatic decision should be made on the merits of the case. They also know that the most time-consuming step in the process is not making the decision, but putting it into effect.

The executive who prides himself on his capacity for making very quick decisions is probably an impulsive and inefficient one, because no important decision is ever so urgent that it cannot wait for an analysis to be made first.

The principle which an executive has to adopt for generic decisions are virtually the same as those adopted by the great Hippocrates for the diagnosis of diseases over 2,000 years ago. Hippocrates used to make an examination of all the past symptoms and then find out the common factors underlying these symptoms. Based on these common factors, Hippocrates would prescribe his treatment. Effective management decisions and good medical diagnosis virtually follow the same principles. After having first found out the things which are common and not something which is isolated and exceptional, a generic decision is made.

Examples of Strategic Decision-Making

International Telephone & Telegraph Company of America

- An interesting example of decision-making is the case of the giant International Telephone and Telegraph Company of America. In most countries of the world, the telephone system is run as one organization in the state because it is not convenient to have two separate telephone systems working side by side. Some of the strategic decisions taken by the Company to avoid becoming nationalized are interesting.

- They are determined to give the best possible service, no matter what the cost.

- They make a deliberate policy to make obsolete every present method, no matter how efficient or profitable it may be. This they do in order to make sure that their customers will always have the latest and the best in communication equipment. These basic beliefs have permeated the whole organization. ITT has always striven for betterment. Not improvement of the present, not defensive research, but always striving to destroy the present, and work on something new and better.

These are some of the strategic decisions that have helped keep the ITT independent and not government owned for so long.

Automobile Manufacturers and Quality

Certain automobile manufacturers laid down standards of performance and excellence, and they refused to budge one iota from them no matter what the cost. So even if a minor blemish was found in any of their vehicles, they recalled the whole lot of automobiles and corrected the defect. And all his was done at great cost to the organization itself. This ties up with the strategic decision of the organization that, above all else, the products of that company must have a reputation for excellence.

Sloan of General Motors

Another example of a strategic decision was that of Sloan of General Motors. When he took charge of the General Motors organization, it consisted of a number of separate units that were almost completely autonomous and headed by strong personalities. Sloan's strategic decision was to preserve the autonomy of these separate units and to give them as free a hand as possible, with plenty of opportunities to use their talents. But all this he held together with a strong and powerful central group that gave overall directions and guidance to these almost autonomous units.

Automobile Accidents

The design of automobiles is another example. It was realized, after an examination of the statistics of automobile accidents, that only a small proportion of people are accident prone: that most car owners do not have accidents. This made people realize that no matter how good the road safety measures might be, the accident prone people will always become involved in automobile accidents. These facts led to a complete revolution in the design of cars. It led to all cars being designed on the assumption that they would actually have an accident, and so they were designed especially to minimize the effect of accidents.

McNamara and Inventory Control

An example where a decision based on averages can lead to a wrong conclusion was brought out by the famous McNamara in the case of inventory control for the US Defence Department. He realized that out of the hundreds of thousands of items of inventory of the Defence Department only about six per cent were of real significance, both in terms of value and importance. So he ordered that all concentration be centred on this six per cent. All the other ninety-four per cent of inventory were dealt with on the basis of average consumption of a number of months. Here is a good example of a strategic decision based on management by exception, where attention is not 'spread' but devoted to the areas where it really matters.

Some People Cannot Keep Still

They just have to do something all the time. Not only is this irritating to others but it can also land them in a lot of trouble. Take decisions. One of the alternatives in the decision-making process is to do nothing at all. This might be the best in the circumstances. A decision in management can be likened to one in surgery. A good surgeon will never operate unless it is necessary. So it is in decision-making. Why make a decision if it is not going to improve things?

Things can sometimes go completely wrong because someone has just refused to consider the alternative of doing nothing. There was the instance of a large section in a factory which had two extra men for many years. The decision to remove these two men caused an uproar which cost far more than if the two men had remained where they were in the first place.

A good decision maker should always ask the question 'What will happen if nothing is done?' There is the example of an executive who had made a first-class decision and saved the company an enormous amount of money. But together with this decision, he made a relatively minor decision on some savings on laundry charges for employees' uniforms. This upset everyone. This

saving on laundry charges was relatively minor but actually it was this decision that was remembered, not the big saving which the executive made after careful work and thinking. Hence, sometimes it is better not to make any changes at all, but to leave things as they are. If only the executive had learnt the importance of this.

In the Middle of the Pacific . . .

. . . you are as alone as that when it comes to taking a decision. Decision-making is a lonely function. The boss may have all the available facts, all the advice, all the data. He can take opinions from as many persons as he likes, but in the last analysis, it is he, and he alone, who has to make the final decision. So you see, the final act of decision-making is really a lonely function — as lonely as being on a desert island in the Pacific.

The Computer and Decisions

There is a lot of loose thinking about what a computer can and cannot do. The salient point to remember is that a computer cannot think, it cannot weigh up alternatives intuitively. It cannot take risks, it cannot make a judgement on various conflicting opinions. These are matters which only the human brain can do. Not the computer. What a computer can do is to follow instructions and it can do this quickly and accurately. But these instructions must be given to them by the human mind. The computer cannot make decisions. It does, in fact, what its name implies — it computes.

In addition, a computer can store enormous quantities of information, and, according to the instructions given to it, can bring out this information in whatever form required and at a speed of a millionth of a second. A computer, properly used, can save an executive valuable time; time which he would otherwise spend sorting out masses of data and figures. A computer does this work at very great speed. Geniuses of the old days, people like Newton and Galileo, were compelled to spend a great deal of time working on relatively routine calculations to prove their points. Sometimes these calculations would take over a year. Now this is where a computer will be enormously useful — it can work out these calculations in a matter of a few minutes, and will have enabled far more use to be made of the genius of Newton and Galileo. A computer gives information quickly and accurately and this is important because speedy and accurate information is a major factor in helping a factory run efficiently. For example, speedy information can help considerably in bringing down inventories and ensuring that there are no last minute hold-ups owing to lack of materials.

A computer is of great help to management to schedule and monitor the progress of work on the hundreds of machine tools which one has in an average works. It helps to ensure that they are all kept working and usefully employed. If information about the work done of each machine is available on a daily basis, it is clearly of great help to an executive for making decisions. This is especially important when changes and improvisations have to be made, because the implications of the revised decisions can be known straightaway with the aid of the computer. All this is very useful for arriving at decisions and enables expensive plant and machinery to be more fully utilized.

The thing to remember, however, is that a computer can only handle common or generic situations — things which happen over and over again, — and it can draw conclusions from them depending on what it has been instructed to do. But when you get an exceptional case, that is where one has to be careful with the computer. The conclusion it arrives at for the generic case cannot, of course, be used for the exceptional case.

12

The Underdog

Our industrial world is highly mechanized and automated. We are tempted to believe that our machines matter more than our men and women. So we need to be reminded sometimes that the most expensive computer is a far simpler device than the human brain. This being so, it is odd that we should pay relatively little attention to human problems. We are apt to treat human beings as machines of the cheaper sort, all alike and expendable. But that is not the best way to treat the people we employ. If they are to give good service, they must be treated as individuals, as folks who have their own feelings and problems. They are not machines and we would do wrong to treat them as machines. Their work can be affected by personal worries. They often find the work unrewarding and dull. There are often moments of friction, as when someone is wrongly blamed for idleness or neglect. People will always grumble in any case, perhaps as an assertion of their individuality. So the first task of managers is to know as many as possible of their employees by name. The second is to build up rather than destroy the individual's self-respect. The third is to remember that the work force is more important than the plant.

Having gone so far to meet the needs of the underdog, we have to guard against going too far in that direction. That people matter more than machines is true. The mistake some idealists make is to believe that the factory exists to provide employment

158

on generous terms and that nothing else matters. That idea is nonsense. The factory exists to provide the world with shoes or bicycles or radio sets, and its efficiency is to be measured by its success in producing goods of excellent quality at the lowest price, consistent with showing a profit. The welfare of the employees is important, but not as important as the profits, without which the enterprise will fail, throwing everyone out of work. An organization which exists for the benefit of its members is at once selfish and feeble. To produce good shoes cheaply is a noble object; to pay high wages so as to keep people quiet is foolish from the outset and will lead to disaster. To be content, people must have pride in their work.

A Cog in a Wheel

There may be hundreds of workers in your factory. But remember that the basic need for each of these hundreds of men and women is to be recognized as an individual. Each worker wants to feel that he means something in the organization and that he's not just a cog in a machine.

Of Course, His Work Is Affected

He has had an argument with his wife and these are the masses of overdue bills; anything which affects his mental attitude is bound to affect his work. It certainly increases the chances of errors and accidents. Watch out for this. Try to find out the reasons for bad work first. You'll then be in a much better position to put things right.

Like Hell . . .

. . . no matter how good they have it, human beings are never content. They will always complain. The important thing is not to get hot and bothered, even if the complaints are directed against you. But it is never easy. And many people end up living on tranquillizers simply because they don't realize that human beings will always complain — even if they've never had it so good before.

Even in His Sleep . . .

. . . Bill has nightmares about his work. His supervisor has made his job so deadly dull that poor Bill even pulls levers in his sleep. There is no break in his monotonous day-to-day routine. It's the supervisor's fault. He has it in his power to make every job much more interesting.

We Are Born with It . . .

. . . right from the start, with a big streak of vanity. We all love to criticize others and we do it often. But if we are being criticized even a little bit, we simply hate it. Of course, we think there is nothing we ourselves do which is wrong! Watch out for this. And do be careful when you criticize.

Craving for Meat

It's all very well for a dog. But ordinary people such as you and I also have cravings, and one of the most important is the hunger

161

for recognition. We just crave for attention and you can be sure that if we have plenty of recognition, we will do our job far better. It doesn't take much time or effort to show appreciation. It's one of those little touches that make all the difference.

What Are the Most Important Assets?

Factory buildings? Expensive plant? Up-to-date equipment? There is no question about it — the most important assets of any business are its human assets. It is true a manager has to deal with machinery, buildings and inventories. But it is even more true that he can only deal with these assets through people. That is why it is so important for him to look after his people well. He should reward them justly, help them to progress, and keep them fully informed. All this contributes towards making his most valuable assets even more valuable.

More for Less

It is quite wrong to suppose that ordinary men and women want only the highest possible wages for working the fewest possible hours. They want to be paid enough and they want to be paid as much as other people doing roughly similar work. But they also want to feel that the work is worthwhile. They would like to be able to say: 'Our firm gives the best value for money,' 'We never produce anything to be ashamed of,', and 'No other factory does as good a job.'

It Happens Often . . .

. . . far more than most of us imagine. People are blamed before all the facts are ascertained. In nine cases out of ten a wrong decision is made because some of the facts are not properly known. How could Bill possibly have done the job three weeks ago when he was away on leave for six weeks?

What's More Important . . .

. . . making money or service? Any enterprise that is only obsessed with the idea of making big profits usually ends up with a loss. Because something higher than money is essential. No matter what type of organization you are in, unless real service is given or a good product is made, you can never have high morale or a healthy feeling of pride in the organization.

But the significant thing is that, in the long run, the highest profits are also made by an organization which has a good research and development section, an organization which insists on the highest standards of quality no matter what the cost, usually ends up doing well financially.

13

Human Relations

Self-respect is essential, but the morale of the men and women you employ is upheld and raised by the consideration you show towards them. There is no other area in which so small an effort achieves so great a result. It all begins with putting yourself in the other man's shoes. What does it feel like to be tending a lathe or, indeed, sweeping the floor? The first rule is to know everyone by name. The second rule is to know something about everyone, enough to inquire about a wife's health, a child's success, a cricket score or football result. The third rule is to listen patiently and avoid giving the ready-made, meaningless reply. Don't threaten or lose your temper and think carefully before you reprimand. Your purpose in speaking is not to relieve your feelings, but to bring about an improvement in the work. Choose your words with this aim in view. Think before you say anything and prepare the way before you criticize. Before passing any comment, Quakers in England used to ask themselves: 'Is it true? Is it necessary? Is it kind?' Without pretending to the same ethical standards, and with no more lofty aim than to see the work done efficiently, we might well ask ourselves the same questions before we let fly. Another point to remember is this: if you shout angrily, you may succeed in frightening people but you will then be unable to teach them anything until the following day. A final point: human relations with warm feelings and pleasant words are 'entirely meaningless if the set-up is badly organized and if people are not in a position to make their contribution and to work in relation with each other. In other words, you cannot have good human relations without a good organization. On the other hand, an occasional angry word will certainly not disturb a relationship that accomplishes something and produces results.

In the Other Fellow's Shoes

Why don't you try sometimes to put yourself in the other fellow's shoes. That'll help you to get the right approach to a problem. Try to visualize the reaction of the other man. You'll be surprised at the results. It will enable you to handle your own problems more effectively.

What a Difference They Make . . .

. . . these little courtesies. And they cost so little by way of effort. But they make a lot of difference to the people with whom we work everyday. Many of us utter little more than a preoccupied grunt among our own people. With strangers, we are all smiles and courtesy. But which people matter more, the casual visitors or the folks with whom we are with everyday?

What is the Most Important Word . . .

. . . in the dictionary? It's the sound of your name. And how buck you feel when someone remembers it. It certainly makes you like him, doesn't it? And how small you feel if someone who should have remembered, forgets your name. 'Hey, you' is said by more people than you imagine. It's certainly worth taking pains to remember a person's name. For most people, their names are the most important word in the world.

The Little Touches . . .

. . . there's no question about it. It's the little touches that make
all the difference. If one of your men is away sick, inquire about
his health when he comes back. If he has a pimple on his nose, ask
him about it. If he takes leave to attend to his sick wife, the supervisor must realize what this leave application means to the man
who makes it. Inquire about her health. It does not take too much
time or effort. It's just a question of being thoughtful. But these
little touches certainly make all the difference.

Listen Patiently

The best way to handle complaints is simply to listen patiently
and attentively. A man often only wants to get something off his
chest.

Ready-made Suits

You find that they do always not fit. It's the same with ready-made answers. When someone brings a problem to you, don't give him a quick ready-made answer, even if you know it's the right one. Help him to think out the answer for himself. Let him work out his own solution. It's far better this way than giving him the answer straightaway. You will never find a faster way of making people more efficient.

Eat It . . .

. . . that's the worst about threats. We threaten without thinking, and in ninety-nine cases out of a hundred, we have to eat our threats simply because we just cannot carry them out. So don't threaten. Because when you have to eat your threats, it's very humiliating. It doesn't do you or anybody any good.

Pave the Way

This is what you must do before you criticize anybody. If people have done something the wrong way and even if they know that they are in the wrong, they will resent it bitterly if you tell them so. First talk about a neutral subject. Then find something you can praise. Pave the way. Then people will take criticism willingly. Otherwise, they will fight to the last to prove that black is white.

Being Psychoanalysed . . .

. . . we can all do with a bit of it sometimes. For example, why do we criticize? If it's because we want people to do better work in future, it is all well and good. But is that the real reason? Are we sure that we don't do it just to make people feel foolish and small? Analyze your motives. It will help you a lot.

Let It Simmer . . .

. . . and the soup will be excellent. But do you know that in your ordinary day-to-day life, it also does a lot of good if you let things simmer. A delay of a day or two seldom does any harm. But if you do a thing immediately and in anger and retort with a furious reply, the damage done may be enormous. And it will take months of hard work to put things right again. So when you feel strongly about something, play it cool. Let things simmer a little.

Troubled Waters . . .

. . . there's certainly a lot of excitement around. It happens very often, but you will never get anything settled in such a state. That's where a good supervisor comes in. He pours oil on troubled waters, he calms everyone down. Only then can good sense prevail.

14

Training

The advent of the computer has made management something of a science and the manager something of a scientist. There is in our work a new element of precise calculation and knowledgeable forecast and this is all very beneficial. The danger in this, however, is to make the manager more remote from the man on the conveyor belt. There was a time when the employer (the original owner of the firm) was portrayed in cartoons as a man expensively dressed, smoking a fat cigar and holding a glass of champagne. He did not care, it was suggested, whether his employees were starving so long as he could himself live in luxury. The caricature may have been unfair but he was shown at least as a human being; and his weaknesses, whether for race meetings or pretty girls, were exactly those his employees would have liked if they could afford them. There was nothing mysterious about that ogre. He was merely a man who possessed what everyone else wanted. The manager who today assumes the white overall of the scientist is far less human and far more remote. There is no reason to think that he enjoys great luxury or maintains a harem. But neither have we the least idea about what he is talking. He retreats behind a smoke-screen of computerized figures, economic theories and scientific equations. The gulf between him and the wage earner is no longer social but intellectual, and that is the deepest gulf of all.

This situation is made worse by today's rapid changes in ownership. Company A is acquired this week by Company B, which is taken over next week by Corporation C. All these changes may be advantageous or even necessary for technical reasons, but the final result can be that the working man does not even know his employer by name. He works for Company A, which he knows to be a subsidiary of Company B and he has heard something about Company B being sold, but he does not know to whom or what. Who, then, is the Boss? Well, it used to be Mr Bedrock, but he was succeeded by Mr Passerby, who was replaced by Dr Intransit. Is he still the Managing Director or is he now Executive Vice-President of the Main Board? We heard that he was to go or he may have gone. There was another name mentioned, Mr Vanishing, but that might have been a rumour. Dr Intransit was certainly the Boss at one time — we saw his signature on a notice — but we never actually saw him. Nor do we know where his office is except that it is somewhere beyond the computer department. We remember seeing the Works Manager, but he answers every question by a reference to the Board and its policy. But who are the directors these days? We used to know several of them at least by name, but there were changes last year and there have been other changes since. To the question, therefore 'Who is the Boss,' our answer must be that we have no idea.

To the problems raised by automation, rationalization and by the application of science, our answer lies in managerial training. The scientific thought which goes into production and marketing must now be applied to man-management and leadership. There are born leaders but these are few. The rest of us have to learn, partly from lectures and discussion, partly from books on management and partly again from experience. There are people in any organization who refuse to learn, but those worth promoting are always learning. These are the men and women who should be moved around from one department to another, gaining a good knowledge of the business as a whole.

Some people may say that the tremendous importance given these days to liking people and being kind to people is being exaggerated. You do sometimes get a chief executive who does not like people. He does not help them. He seems to dislike them. He is cold, unpleasant and demanding. But curiously enough, this kind of chief executive sometimes trains more people than anyone else, because he only considers what is right and not who is right.

One helpful quality which cannot be derived from training is a sense of humour. Most of us can, in fact, see the funny side of things but we sometimes fail to realize that a sense of humour is important. It is valuable, to begin with, in saving us from being stupidly angry about some trifling mishap. Some damage may have been done, but we see the funny side of it and merely laugh. It is more valuable in another way. Suppose there is friction between two men, both of them valuable, and others are taking sides. There are all the makings of a serious quarrel with bad feelings that could last for years. The best immediate cure is a joke which will relieve the tension and make people forget the cause of the dispute. We cannot always think of a joke in time but we do well to cultivate our sense of humour and try to have a stock of useful jokes. At a moment of crisis a joke may save the situation, proving more valuable than the most eloquent plea for co-operation, tolerance and common sense.

Scientific Management Needed

Maybe his business is flourishing; maybe he doesn't believe in management techniques. But he would certainly do much better if he adopted modern methods of managment:

- Firstly, he should learn to delegate his work because the job of management is far too extensive for any one man to do by himself. Running an enterprise is entirely different from running one's own personal investments and properties.

- A major requirement in managing people is to fix objectives for each one of them: to have a proper structure of management. Everyone must know exactly what they have to do and to whom they must report.

- An executive must plan ahead and make budgets. He must always watch to see how actual results compare with budgets

or plans for the future. Unless everything is budgeted or planned for, there is bound to be waste.

- Matters must not be left to chance and intuition. A manager must ensure that things turn out the way he wants them to happen.

- He must know how to motivate people, how to make them want to work. And to accomplish this, he must know how to communicate with them.

- The next basic element in the work of a manager is that of measurement. Norms should be fixed for the work of every one. A manager should not only see that the work of each person fits in with the performance of the whole organization, but he should also ensure the work of each individual is in keeping with the work allotted to him.

177

- Finally, a manager must develop people. This is perhaps his main job. Not only will this make his job easier but he will have people ready to take over from him when there is an opportunity for promotion to a higher post.

Every manager, whether he knows it or not, does most of the things which we have mentioned above. Some do them well. Some do them wretchedly. You may not become an Alfred Sloan if you do them well. But they will certainly be of great help to you.

But Why Not in Leadership?

An enormous amount of time and money is spent training executives in their own specialized subjects such as chemistry, engineering, physics, law and accountancy, but supervision is perhaps the most important part of their work. And training for that seems to be almost entirely forgotten. The trouble is that executives tend to assume that they know all that needs to be known about supervision and dealing with people.

Companies do not hesitate to provide large sums of money for improving the technical knowledge of their staff. But they seldom realize that it would pay them as well, if not more, to devote the same amount of effort and money to research on human relations. It is surprising, isn't it? Especially since the average executive spends at least seventy-five per cent of his time just dealing with people.

There are, of course, born leaders but these are relatively few. It is possible, however, to learn the habits and thoughts which will in time make capable managers. Leadership is something which can be learnt and considerably improved upon by studying and learning from the experience of others and by following certain practices. Skill in leadership is normally something that does not come by itself except in rare cases.

One of Them . . .

. . . may be a Napoleon, an Einstein, a Shakespeare or a Julius Caesar. But people can only be born that way. Even with the best training and coaching in the whole world, you can never make a Napoleon or an Einstein.

But with the average ordinary people, no matter how much or how little ability they may have at birth, there's no question that with proper training, they can improve. Management conferences, seminars, training courses and talking to others can all help to increase competence. You can never have too much of training. No matter how good or bad you are, proper training will always make you just that much better.

Just as a Baby . . .

. . . has to be properly fed, it is equally important that executives are constantly nourished so that they grow and develop.

- One important source of food is for the manager to send his executives to other factories, seminars and conferences. There they will exchange ideas with their counterparts who have similar responsibilities.

- Another source of learning is the enormous amount of literature which comes out every month. The latest thinking on management practices is always put into writing and this should be made available at all times.

- Contact with the arts, literature and music is another important form of nourishment. It helps to give one a balanced view; it places one's values in the right perspective.

- One needs experience to be a manager. Nothing is as pathetic as the young man who has learnt business management in a school and believes himself to be qualified to manage people and to run things. He can do any amount of damage if he is not careful.

It Never Comes Back . . .

. . . and that's time. We all have just so much of it. We can just waste it, or we can enrich our lives with it. Most of us spend our time on current things; ordinary day-to-day things which are

TIME BEING USED UP

TIME BEING INVESTED

necessary to get a job done. Some people think that it is much better to work hard at their everyday jobs than to attend lectures, training classes and seminars where they can absorb fresh knowledge and ideas. They do not seem to realize that if time is properly invested, it will put them in a position far more effective than where they are. Not only will the quality of their work become infinitely better but they will work with greater satisfaction.

It Isn't Enough to Have a Policy: It Must Be Carried Out

It is one thing to have a policy laid down on paper, but it is an entirely different matter to ensure that the policy is carried out. For example, many companies pride themselves on their executive development schemes. Yet how many of their senior executives actually get down to details and check whether their men are in fact being developed?

Never Twice

Make a mistake once. That's natural; it's healthy. It means that

people are willing to take the initiative, but if the same mistake is made again, then you should start worrying. It means that the previous mistake was not investigated. It was not brought to the notice of the man who made it. Supervision has obviously slipped up somewhere.

The finest teacher is a mistake — we should learn from it, and not repeat it.

Keep Your Cool

There are always possible sources of friction when men are at work. The previous shift failed to tidy up before it quit. Some of those taking over are late. Men can belong to different trade unions with different rules. People can come from different parts of the country and have different ideas about how the work should be done. In a moment of stress words can be exchanged and can even be misunderstood. From words we go on to blows and the whole place can be in an uproar before anyone has time to intervene. Someone at this stage may call the police and next day the incident will be described in the local newspaper as a riot inspired by communists! This sort of report, often exaggerated, does the firm no good. It would be far better to end the trouble before it really begins.

Help! Police!

The worst way to end a dispute is to call in the police. It is far better to end the disturbance by an appeal to reason. Better still crack a joke, one which makes the quarrelling men see that they are behaving childishly. In this instance the boss and the supervisor have acted swiftly and effectively. They have staged a caricature of the quarrel and the men have seen the humour of it. The crisis is over and the foreman can now inquire into the causes of the dispute. The same gambit will not always succeed, but the essential idea is sound. People must be shown that they are making themselves ridiculous.

Periodic Get-togethers

- Give them only information and the facts. Never get drawn into any discussion during these meetings.

- After you have given them information, receive information from the people attending and answer any questions they may put. But only factual stuff. Again, remember, avoid discussion because that will go on and on and on.

- Where there's a problem to be solved, there should be a separate meeting with only those people who are directly concerned.

- The meeting should always start at the same time and be held at the same place.

- For certain types of meetings, it might even be worthwhile having them with everyone standing to make sure that they don't get too prolonged.

Why Do We Have Meetings?

- Is it because we want a decision?

- Do we want to inform?

- Do we want to make clear to ourselves what we should be doing? A good leader is always clear in his mind about the objectives of a meeting and at the end of the meeting he usually goes back to the opening statement and relates the final conclusion to the original intention of the meeting. Unless the objectives of a meeting are clear, much time is wasted in just talk. At a meeting everyone must address the chair and only the chair — and only one man can talk at a time.

15

Think Ahead

All who are on the payroll should do their best to see that each day's work is properly done. It is the special task of management to look beyond the day's work and think about potential future problems. Next year's situation may not be the same. In five years' time, the scene may be completely transformed, bringing new opportunities and new dangers. It is vital, therefore, for the managers to think ahead. If they are to do this they must, first of all, give themselves time to think. If they are frantically busy all day and exhausted before they leave the office, they have failed in their task of organization. They will make bad decisions when tired, as for example, in giving up some project which, with persistence, might have succeeded. They will reject some proposal because of some mistake in detail. They will reach hasty conclusions towards the end of the day and then change their minds, making other people work late. People begin the next day tired and cross with the result that more mistakes follow, some in figures and some in policy. Errors accumulate — all the fault of a bad organization which gives the management no time to look ahead.

What is wrong with the organization? In most instances (not in all), the firm is over-centralized. Problems which should have been solved at the middle level have been heaped on the desk of the chief executive. The fault is his. He tries to do too much and the penalty is twofold: overwork for him and arrested development among his executives. It is this overwork which prevents thinking ahead and the result could be the ruin of the firm.

It is not enough to do the day's work. It is not enough to keep level with one's competitors. The good leader looks to the future and chooses his own line, foreseeing the problem and defining the goal. Nor is that the ultimate test of leadership, for while there must be a plan the situation is unlikely to remain the same. So the plan must be flexible since priorities are likely to alter. But of this we can be sure: the man with enough imagination to draw up plan A is the very man to have Plan B up his sleeve and ready for an emergency. The language of business is money and the plans we draw up are largely, though not entirely, in the form of budgets for future investment. These have to be realistic if they are to be useful and simply expressed if they are to be understood. The language of accountancy is apt to obscure and confuse our purpose. We would do better to avoid any air of mystery and tell people plainly what has to be done.

The success of a business rests largely on the morale of the wage earners and this rests, in turn, on the authority of those in control. Authority, the basic attribute of leadership, comprises the two elements of power and reputation. Power by itself is fragile and reputation by itself is impotent. Join the two and the holder of an important office brings to it the reputation he has already earned before appointment. In terms of reputation, each holder of a significant post either adds to its invisible bank balance or draws upon it. Should there be a succession of non-entities, the account is overdrawn and the office loses all significance, nothing remaining but an empty and meaningless title. Where, however, there is a succession of men with a well-earned reputation, the office they have held gains in consequence. And nothing does more for their reputation than the fact that they always look ahead, foreseeing both opportunities and dangers. Under a farsighted leader the rank and file have a feeling of security. They work better under the leader they have learnt to trust. They will accept authority, whereas they resent mere power. As we near the top, our aim must always be to establish the sort of reputation which will complement the power with which we may be entrusted. And once our authority has been established, our goals will be achieved.

The First Thing in the Morning . . .

. . . at least half an hour should be devoted just to planning your work for the day. Most executives have a tendency to rush in and do the first job that comes to hand: telephones, meetings, answering queries, and so it goes on for the whole day. Pause for a while in the morning and just plan the priorities of your work. It could be the most useful part of your day:

- Does everyone in the organization know who is answerable to whom?

- Have the letters in the Grievance File been properly answered?

- Has X been congratulated on the good job which he did last week?

- Has the notice regarding the partial lay-off in A Department been properly worded so that the reasons for the lay-off can be clearly understood by everyone?

- Has executive Y who is very sick in hospital been visited?

- Is the actual performance of the company keeping in line with the budget or the plan?

- Is enough finance available for the completion of factory extension A which is scheduled to begin production by the end of the financial year?

These are some of the tasks for which an executive is paid — they are some of the tasks on which he should concentrate and not the first thing that comes in the In-tray.

189

Don't Give Up

He is bound to succeed in the end if he keeps on at it! It doesn't matter how many times you fail. Remember what happened to King Bruce of Scotland. It's not the brilliant fellow that gets on in the long run, but the fellow that has the capacity and the patience for going at it again and again and not giving up. Was it not Thomas Edison who said that 'Genius is one per cent inspiration and ninety-nine per cent perspiration'?

An Exquisite Painting

But see how worked up he is! A very slight defect in the painting of the toe nails and this wonderful piece of art is summarily rejected. Poor girl! But in ordinary life too you will be surprised at the number of good ideas which come to nothing because someone has found a minor defect. Watch out for this.

Jumping to Conclusions

That's what many of us do so often without first trying to master all the facts.

Take highly qualified personnel. Some people have an aversion to engage them because they have had some unfortunate experience with qualified people in the past. So to them, all highly qualified personnel are useless.

Take committee meetings. Some people have had very trying experiences in committees which wasted a lot of time and accomplished nothing.

Similarly, some people believe in decentralization in organization and others in centralization. These beliefs are based on their

191

past experience. But this experience might not have been at all representative. So take care before you jump to conclusions.

Straightening It Out

This is all very well in a forge shop. There you have to straighten out pieces of metal. But in a factory, you have to plan well ahead so that you anticipate and avoid mistakes and don't get into a mess which you'll have to straighten out later. A little time spent thinking clearly right from the beginning will avoid a lot of unnecessary and time-consuming patching up and straightening out later on.

Look What Time it is

It is 9.30 p.m. And they are all hard at it preparing a statement that is wanted 'higher up'. This happens all too often. The boss in the office or maybe someone even higher up at headquarters decides that he wants some information very urgently. So everyone is kept working up to midnight trying to get it. Naturally

there is tension; and naturally people collapse. Why can't the bosses look ahead a little? These unnecessary spurts of fever pitch activity do no good to anyone.

Don't Let Day-to-Day Pressures Determine Your Work: Plan It

Wherever you have organizations, inevitably there is a need to make decisions at some time or other. The important thing in management is that a decision must never be forced by day-to-day pressures, but must be arrived at after careful planning and forethought. A decision about the future plans of an organization can always be postponed. It does not have to be made today or tomorrow or even in the next month. But many of the day-to-day pressures cannot be postponed.

What often happens in many organizations is that they continuously work under pressure, with the result that planning about the future of their organization is postponed indefinitely. This, of course, is disastrous in the long run. An organization simply must not be run by day-to-day pressures. It is essential to get time to plan for the future quietly and unhurriedly.

193

Think of the Future: The Past is Over and Done With

- Always think ahead and towards the future, and not so much about the past, or about what is happening today.

- Concentrate on the opportunities, rather than on the difficulties of a problem.

- Tackle a problem in your own way, as you think best and not necessarily in a manner in which others have been doing it.

- Always set your sights high and aim for something that will really make a big difference. This is far better than doing the usual thing or something which is easy to do.

- The work of most executives today is really determined by decisions that have been made in the past. But this is something which should be avoided as far as possible. The work of executives should be to plan and decide things for the future. It may be to give up a product altogether, or to concentrate on the more important lines, or perhaps to make an improvement on an existing line, or maybe to change the pattern of the organization so as to make things work more smoothly. Executives should spend much more time thinking about the future than about today. This is the best way to avoid crises and haphazard work.

It Doesn't Take More Time to Bring Out Something Entirely New

In business, the important thing is not so much to improve existing products but to set your sights on something entirely new, something that will lead to a breakthrough. That is how great things have been achieved in the past and will be achieved in the future. Forget the past and set your sights on something new and much better. Why improve and adapt something which you already have. It does not take much more energy and time to work out something entirely new and far better. Remember most

194

products have a life cycle. Drop them like hot bricks preferably when they are at their peak — and then think out something new.

Don't Be an 'Also Ran' . . .

. . . it's fatal. Management must continually be on the look-out for new ideas and for improvements. There are many things which managers in government, in business, in schools or in hospitals would like to do but cannot. They know that their bosses or the rules won't allow them to make the necessary changes. The result is that they often waste their time and energy complaining about the things which they cannot do anything about. But what is important is that, in most cases, in spite of all the restraints, there are a number of things which can be done and are worth doing. Whilst an inefficient manager complains about the things that cannot be done, it is the able manager who goes right ahead and does the things which can be done. One often finds that the executives who complain that people and rules won't let them do

what they want are the ones who use this as an alibi for inertia and inefficency. There are always worthwhile things which an executive can do if he really puts his mind to it. The question he should always ask is 'What can I do?' and not 'What can I *not* do?' This goes for people at all levels of an organization.

A manager must strive to do things better than others and not merely to imitate them. The 'Also Ran' type of manager just wants to carry on. He only wishes to benefit from the efforts of others. He just follows the leader, he imitates others. What one wants is a real leader, a person with the determination to follow the right course of action according to his own thinking. A leader who has the vision to look right ahead into the future and direct his organization's efforts towards it: a man who is prepared to take positive action on present circumstances which might be most unfavourable as long as he is convinced that his present action will favour his long term aims.

Even a Guess Estimate . . .

. . . is better than no estimate at all. It is far better to work with even imperfect guesses than to be static and unimaginative. The

greater the uncertainty of the future the more a company needs to probe into it and anticipate future changes. This is the secret of most go-ahead companies. By constantly looking into the future and revising estimates again and again, they are able to anticipate events and even determine them. They are not caught unawares: they are able to deal with new developments.

The Tasks of Management Have Changed

Human beings have not altered much in the course of recorded history. They have not grown in intellectual stature or maturity. The Bible is still the measure of a man's stature. Aeschylus and Shakespeare still provide the best textbooks of psychology and sociology. Socrates and St Thomas Aquinas still represent the high watermarks of human intellect.

But organizations have grown enormously over the years and have become much more complex. How then can we accomplish the new tasks of running these huge organizations with the same sort of men? The tasks of the executive have already been discussed in the book in some detail. The position is summarized on the next page.

- Management by objectives and self-control is a much better way of getting things done than management by domination by a boss.

- An executive must take calculated risks.

- He must make as few decisions as possible. The ones he makes should be strategic decisions.

- He must build up an integrated team out of what otherwise might have been a mere mob.

- He must measure and analyse each person's performance against estimates.

- He must communicate quickly and clearly.

- He must motivate people.

- He must see the business as a whole.

- He must work on principles and concepts: not on hunches or intuition.

- He must always aim to simplify.

- He must choose, develop and train his staff, including those who will eventually replace him.

An executive has to make an organization a productive entity which turns out more than the sum of the resources put into it. To a certain extent, it can be likened to a symphony orchestra: the conductor attempts to get everything he can out of a composition; he welds each and every member of the orchestra together so that they perform as one unified team. The executive has to do the same, but the big difference is that he is both the composer as well as the conductor and he also has to look ahead; he has to think about the long term plans of the organization, whilst the conductor's task is only the interpretation of the score before him.